INSANE FOR THE LIGHT

INSANE
for the
LIGHT

|||||||||||||||||||||||||||||||

*A Spirituality for
Our Wisdom Years*

RONALD
ROLHEISER

IMAGE

Image

An imprint of the Penguin Random House Christian Publishing Group,
a division of Penguin Random House LLC
1745 Broadway, New York, NY 10019
imagecatholicbooks.com
penguinrandomhouse.com

IMAGE with colophon is a registered trademark of
Penguin Random House LLC.

Hardback ISBN 978-0-593-73646-3
International edition ISBN 059373646X
Ebook ISBN 978-0-593-73647-0

The Cataloging-in-Publication Data is on file with the Library of Congress.

Printed in the United States of America on acid-free paper

1st Printing

First Edition

The authorized representative in the EU for product safety and compliance is
Penguin Random House Ireland, Morrison Chambers, 32 Nassau Street, Dublin
D02 YH68, Ireland. https://eu-contact.penguin.ie

BOOK TEAM: Production editor: Laura K. Wright • Managing editor: Julia
Wallace • Production manager: Mark Maguire • Copy editor: Kathy Mosier •
Proofreaders: Drew Goter, Judy Kiviat

Book design by Susan Turner

For details on special quantity discounts for bulk purchases, contact
specialmarketscms@penguinrandomhouse.com.

For all of you who are struggling with the aging process.
May you become an Elder who brings sanity, a wide perspective,
an honest view of the past, a space of kindness, a space of refuge,
a safe place to grieve, and a subversive joy into a room.

The Holy Longing

Tell a wise person, or else keep silent,
because the mass man will mock it right away.
I praise what is truly alive,
what longs to be burned to death.

In the calm water of the love-nights,
where you were begotten, where you have begotten,
a strange feeling comes over you,
when you see the silent candle burning.

Now you are no longer caught in the obsession with darkness,
and a desire for higher love-making sweeps you upward.

Distance does not make you falter.
Now, arriving in magic, flying,
and finally, insane for the light,
you are the butterfly and you are gone.
And so long as you haven't experienced this: to die and so to grow,
you are only a troubled guest on the dark earth.

—Johann Wolfgang von Goethe
Translated from the German by Robert Bly

CONTENTS

PREFACE

Insane for the Light

WHEN RACHEL NAOMI REMEN WAS FOURTEEN YEARS OLD, SHE sometimes worked as a volunteer companion at a nursing home for the aged. One particular Saturday she was assigned to spend the morning with a ninety-six-year-old woman who had not spoken for a year. Initially, on entering the room, Rachel tried to engage the old woman, but the woman ignored every approach and just stared out the window. From time to time, Rachel would make a new attempt to engage her, but she was always ignored. Finally, she gave up and simply waited until a bell signaled that her assigned time was up and she could leave.

One day as Rachel was leaving, she asked the woman, "What are you looking at?" When the woman turned to look at her, Rachel saw her face—it was radiant—and the woman replied, "Why, child, I am looking at the Light."

Rachel Naomi Remen was destined to see that exact look again on a human face. She went on to become a pediatrician, and that same rapt expression is the look she sees on the face of a new-born baby when it opens its eyes for the first time to the light.

In his poem "The Holy Longing," Johann Wolfgang von Goethe tells us that if we mature as nature intended, we will one day reach a stage in our lives when we will become genuine Elders, holy old fools, wise Sophias, *sannyasins,* holy beggars who, having arrived at a certain magic, realize that we are "only a troubled guest on the dark earth" and now become "insane for the light."

One size doesn't fit everyone. This is not just true for clothing; it is also true for spirituality. Our challenges in life change as we age. Spiritual guidance has not always been fully sensitive to this. True, we have always had tailored instruction and activities for children, young people, and people who are raising children, carrying a job, and paying a mortgage, but we have never developed a spirituality for what happens when those years are over.

Why is one needed? Jesus seemingly did not have one. He did not have one set of teachings for the young, another for those in midlife, and still another for the elderly. He just taught. The Sermon on the Mount, the parables, and his invitation to take up his cross are intended in the same way for everyone, regardless of age. But we hear those teachings in different ways at different times in our lives; it's one thing to hear the Sermon on the Mount when you are seven years old, another when you are twenty-seven, and quite another when you are eighty-seven. Jesus's teachings do not change, but we do, and they offer very specific challenges at different times of our lives.

So, how do we receive what Jesus has to say about aging, retirement, the loss of health, and how to prepare to die? Is there a spirituality for our later years articulated in the Gospels?

Yes. But except for a few salient exceptions, Christian spirituality has failed to develop an explicit spirituality for our later years, for how we are meant to be generative in a new way in our senior years and how we are meant to die in a way that is life-giving to others. There is a good reason for this lacuna. Simply put, it was not much needed because up until this last century, most people never lived into old age. For example, in Palestine in Jesus's time, the average life expectancy was thirty to thirty-five years. A century ago in the United States, it was still less than fifty years. When most people in the world died before they reached the age of fifty, there was little cry for a spirituality of aging.

There is such a spirituality in the Gospels. Even though Jesus died at thirty-three, he left us a paradigm of how to age and die. But that paradigm, while healthily infusing and undergirding Christian spirituality in general, was never developed more specifically into a spirituality of aging (with the exception of some of the great Christian mystics).

In terms of an explicit spirituality of aging and dying, what has happened in the two thousand years since Jesus walked the earth? In this specific area, Christian spirituality has been greatly shaped through the centuries by two major influences: the persecutions and martyrdom of the early Christians and the ideals of the Desert Fathers and Mothers.

First, in the time of the persecutions and the early Christian martyrs, the idea developed that the ideal way to age and die was through martyrdom. Later, when Christians were no longer physically martyred, the idea took hold that one could take on a voluntary type of martyrdom by making religious vows of poverty, chastity, and obedience. Adherents of this thinking believed that living in this way taught people all they needed to know, no matter their age. Eventually this idea expanded to mean that anyone who faithfully responded to the duties in his life, regardless of age, would learn everything necessary to come to sanctity through that fidelity. As a famous aphorism put it, "Stay in your cell and it will teach you all you need to know." Understood properly, there's a spirituality of aging and dying inside these notions, but until recently there was little need to draw it out.

A second major influence was the ideal of the Desert Fathers and Mothers. For them, spirituality was a quest to see the face of God, which, as Jesus makes clear, requires one thing: purity of heart. "Blessed are the pure in heart, for they will see God." So for spirituality and discipleship, no matter a person's age, the challenge was always the same: trying to achieve purity of heart. Many of our classic Christian manuals and renowned mystics essentially affirmed this theme. In that context, the question of how to age and die was folded into the overall framework of the continual pursuit of purity of heart.

This was the situation in Roman Catholicism, if not always the case outside it. The Reformation named its own ideals for how a person could be constantly challenged by the Gospels. But no one within any Christian denomination developed an explicit spirituality for aging and giving one's death away. It is noteworthy that while an explicit, developed spirituality of aging and dying did not develop within Christianity, it did within Hinduism and Buddhism.

Happily, today the situation is changing, and we are developing, more and more, some explicit Christian spiritualities of aging and dying. Perhaps due to our aging population, there is now a burgeoning body of literature, both religious and secular, that is addressing the question of aging and dying. These authors, too numerous to mention, include many names already familiar to us: Henri Nouwen, Richard Rohr, Kathleen Dowling Singh, David Brooks, Cardinal Joseph Bernardin, James Hillman, Michael Paul Gallagher, Joan Chittister, Parker Palmer, Marilyn

Chandler McEntyre, Paul Kalanithi, Daniel O'Leary, Erica Jong, Katie Roiphe, and Wilkie and Noreen Au, among others. Coming from a variety of perspectives, each offers insights into what God and nature intend for us in our later years.

In essence, here's the issue today: We are living longer and healthier late in life. It is common today to retire in our early sixties after having raised our children and paid our mortgages. So, what is next, given that we probably have twenty or thirty more years of health and energy left? What are these years for? What are we called to now, beyond loving our grandkids?

Or, to employ a biblical image, when Sarah was seventy years old and Abraham was eighty, God asked them to set out for a foreign place and promised that they would have the heir they had always longed for when they got there. Well, that journey took them twenty years. And then, when Sarah was ninety and Abraham was one hundred, they gave birth to Isaac, the heir they had longed for all their lives. What happened here? How does one have a post-menopausal baby? Literal history here befuddles the mind because it is meant to, but the meaning of this story radically challenges the mind. How are we meant to become pregnant and bring forth a birth that is not biological, long after our hair has turned gray? Moreover, how is this child of our post-menopausal years meant to be our real heir, our real legacy? The metaphor begs for a lot of unpacking—and that is the intent of this book.

The great mystic writer John of the Cross suggests that as human beings, we pass through three major stages in our lives. Initially, we *struggle to get our lives together;* after that, we *struggle to give our lives away;* and finally, in the last stage of our lives, we *struggle to age with grace and give our deaths away as a gift to others.* Christian spirituality has been better at guiding us through the first two struggles than it has at giving us guidance for the third struggle: how to age properly and give our deaths away as a gift.

In my research, teaching, and writing, I have tried to address each of these three struggles in a systematic way. Two previous books offered a Christian vision on how to deal with the first two phases of our lives. *The Holy Longing: The Search for a Christian Spirituality* addressed the first phase, our struggle to get our lives together. A subsequent book, *Sacred Fire: A Vision for a Deeper Human and Christian Maturity,* articulated a vision on how to generatively give our lives away as Christians. This book, *Insane for the Light,* attempts to complete the trilogy in that it addresses the third and final struggle in our lives: how we are meant to age in a way that continues to be generative and how our deaths are meant to be our final gift to others.

I have drawn the title, *Insane for the Light,* from Goethe's poem "The Holy Longing." At a certain point in our lives, he tells us, "a desire for higher love-making" will become our new obsession and eventually will make us "insane for the light." And, in that, we will be able to understand that aging and dying are really just a new birth.

Several years ago, I went with a young colleague to visit a ninety-year-old man whom we both admired because he had aged in such a marvelous way that he radiated nothing but warmth, gratitude, blessing, and humor. At one point, my young colleague said to him, "When I'm your age I want to be like you! What's the secret?" The old man's answer: "Start now!" The purpose of this book is to suggest ways that each of us, no matter our age, might "start now."

Ronald Rolheiser
Oblate School of Theology
San Antonio, Texas

PART ONE

||||||||||||||||||||||||||||||||||

THE SEASONS OF OUR LIVES

T HAT IS WHY I HAVE DECIDED TO STAND UP AND OPEN MY EYES. I have decided to eat and drink in moderation, to sleep as necessary, to write only what contributes toward improving those who read me, to abstain from greed, and never compare myself to my fellows. I have also decided to water my plants and care for an animal. I will visit the sick, I will converse with the lonely, and I will not let much time go by before playing with a child. . . .

I will live for those things according to an ethics of attention and care. And this is how I will arrive at a happy old age, when I will contemplate, humble and proud at the same time, the small but grand orchard that I have cultivated. Life as cult, culture, and cultivation.

ONE

〰〰〰〰〰〰〰〰〰〰〰

Spirituality and the Seasons of Our Lives

For everything there is a season, and a time for every matter under heaven.

Life has its seasons. So do we. We cry as infants, stagger as toddlers, soak up learning from kindergarten to puberty, become painfully restless as our hormones awaken in adolescence, make choices and settle into life as young adults, carry the burdens of duty and mortgages as we mature, retire in late midlife, and then, finally mature, face diminishment and death.

All of this, of course, has been endlessly diagnosed, analyzed, and studied from medical, psychological, sociological, mythical, and religious perspectives. As well, artists, poets, photographers, and biographers have created an aesthetics around it through pictures and stories that highlight the joy, the pathos, and sometimes the mind-numbing ordinariness of the different seasons of our lives. And all of this is helpful. The studies feed the intellect; the aesthetics touch the heart. A healthy Christian discipleship.

Leaning on both the intellect and the heart, we ask this question: How might we distinguish, define, and understand the various seasons of our lives in a way that helps us grow in self-understanding and Christian discipleship?

Following the renowned Spanish mystic John of the Cross, it can be helpful to distinguish *three* major seasons or stages within our lives. John of the Cross, using medieval and mystical terminology, calls these three seasons *the dark night of the senses, proficiency,* and *the dark night of the spirit.* In today's language, we might more aptly call them *the struggle to get our lives together, the struggle to give our lives away,* and *the struggle to age with grace and give our deaths away.*

Admittedly, these stages or seasons of life are fairly obvious. Unless one dies young, everyone has to undergo these three struggles. Each of these struggles involves our whole person: Our spiritual struggle is not separate from our human struggle. Our faith journey and our human journey are one and the same, even if they may seem separate. For all of us, the deeper truth is that the anthropological, the spiritual, the psychological, the emotional, the moral, the sexual, the vocational, and the physical are all part of one and the same person, struggle, and journey. We struggle as human beings, pure and simple. Hence, everyone who reaches full adulthood undergoes these struggles, regardless of whether she senses them as a spiritual struggle.

THE FIRST SEASON: THE STRUGGLE
TO GET OUR LIVES TOGETHER

The struggle to get our lives together might be best illustrated by the commonplace journey most of us make from youth to adulthood, from immaturity to initial maturity. What, in essence, is this initial struggle?

Home is where we start from. We are either born in a home or taken home soon afterward. Then, unless we are scarred by some trauma in our childhood, the next ten to twelve years are normally good, stabilizing, happy, comfortable years. We are at home, content enough with being children, eager to experience things, alert and attentive to most everything, quick to learn, and hopefully comfortable being with our families. But then puberty hits us with a violence powerful enough to rearrange our bodies and emotions quickly and fundamentally. This is not an anomaly but nature's way. Puberty is designed by God and nature to drive us out of our home so that we have to seek a new home, one that we choose and build.

This journey that puberty puts us on is really our first truly personal struggle for individuation. Admittedly, we struggled before that and had to assert ourselves right from the moment of birth to find a place in this world and claim our individuality, but we were able to do this in the protective safety of a cocoon, a home. Puberty sends us packing our bags and setting out along a road on which we must find a new home. It drives us out of our initial home to begin the first major personal struggle in our lives, the struggle to find out who we are and, in that, to find a vocation, a mate, a community, a support system, a maturity, and a meaning for our lives.

In *Sacred Fire,* I highlighted how during that season of our lives, we struggle with some very powerful fires that fill the body, the mind, and the heart so as to make this journey one that is filled with deep restlessness, deep heartache, deep insecurity, and deep danger.

These powerful energies deeply root themselves in one energy that undergirds and fuels all the others—namely, in something the ancient Greeks called "Eros." What is this? The word takes its root from the Greek god of love and sex, Eros, who was the child of Aphrodite, the Greek goddess of love, beauty, pleasure, passion, and procreation. Hence, for the ancient Greeks and for the Neoplatonic philosophers who followed them (and deeply influenced Christian theology), the word "Eros" took on the connotation of all the energies we feel inside us that are connected to love, sex, beauty, pleasure, passion, and creativity. Sadly, today, the word is mostly reduced to the word "erotic" and is identified almost exclusively with sex.

Eros is more than sex. It is the sheer pulse for life that is at the root of every energy inside us, physical and spiritual. In our younger years, particularly in the years from puberty to early midlife, this sheer pulse for life, Eros, is very strong. We see this in the bubbly, lively, noisy, endless energy of young people who, at this stage of their lives, can carry deep wounds and still be bouncy cheerleaders. We see it in the laughter and partying of youth, and we see it as well in their grandiose hopes and dreams. Of itself, it is a beautiful energy, a God-given one. It does make the world go round.

But, like all things powerful, it is not always easy to handle. We also see its gripping power in the struggle of youth to channel sexuality properly; in their pathological restlessness; in their sulky loneliness; in their struggle to sort out its moral energies; in their struggle for meaning, personal identity, significance, and self-worth; and (not least) in their inchoate nostalgia to "come home," to find roots, moral companionship, a soulmate.

A lot can be understood about the energies that drive us from the onset of puberty until midlife by more closely examining the concept of inchoate nostalgia, the desire in us to come home. My younger brother shares this story: In his fifties, he was working in an office with colleagues who were in their twenties and thirties.

One Friday afternoon during break, a number of them were sharing their plans for the weekend. Some were planning to hit the city's nightclubs and restaurants. Others were planning trips to the mountains. Everyone, it seemed, was planning something exciting. When it was my brother's turn, he shared rather sheepishly that on Friday evenings he and his wife (happily married for more than thirty years) usually ordered pizza and watched a movie. "That must sound pretty boring to you," he added. "Not at all," a twentysomething woman said. "You know, we do all the things that we are doing, all the clubs and socials, so that when we are your age, we can be content at home with a pizza and a movie on a Friday night!"

She is right, and her insight can be taken as a summary statement of our struggle to get our lives together. Puberty awakens some very powerful energies inside us, energies that have us deeply restless, struggling with sexuality, dreaming great dreams, and wrestling with great temptations; but, in the end, the intent of all those energies is to bring us home again, to a family, to a vocation, to meaning, to moral companionship, to a soulmate, to pizza and a movie on a Friday night.

This journey to find our way back home again can take ten to twenty years, especially today when it can take a long time to prepare for a career. It also does not come with any guarantees; some people never find their way home again but still at age forty or fifty are struggling with the question, Where am I going with my life? As well, the journey is not without its dangers, particularly given that in most cultures today, we do not have effective initiation rites to turn boys into men and girls into women.

However, most of us do make it home again. After some restless years of adolescence and young adulthood, when we are searching for an identity, a meaning, a life partner, a career, and a job, we one day find ourselves at home again, in a home we have created. We have a house, a partner, children, a mortgage, a job, a career, a vocation, and lots of responsibilities that we have given ourselves over to and that basically define us. The questions that nag us now are not so much "Who am I?" and "Who will love me?" and "What will I do with my life?" but instead "How do I do all this?" and "How do I give myself over to all these responsibilities in a life-giving way?"

Once our focus shifts from worrying about ourselves to concern about being a generative woman or man, we have crossed the first major barrier in terms of human maturity. We have also moved from the first essential struggle in our lives, *the struggle to get our lives together,* to the second essential struggle, *the struggle to give our lives away.* We have also found our way back home again.

THE SECOND SEASON: THE STRUGGLE TO GIVE OUR LIVES AWAY

We do not just wake up one day and find ourselves mature. The transition from immaturity to maturity is gradual, like a change in a weather pattern: One day the forecasts say it will be cloudy all day; a day or two later, they tell us it will be cloudy with intermittent sun; some days later, they tell us it will be sunny but with intermittent clouds; and finally, some days later still, they tell us it will be clear and sunny all day.

Our growth from immaturity to maturity mimics that: Initially we are immature. However, in our adolescence, we are immature but with rays of maturity breaking through. Eventually we become mature but still manifest some immaturity. Unlike a perfectly clear sky, we never quite have maturity without some clouds of immaturity.

Finally, at some point in our lives, we are essentially mature— at least most people are—and that might be described in this way:

To be mature means we have broken the pleasure principle as our fundamental motivation for doing things. It means we have attained an identity wherein we are not forever haunted with questions about who we are and what our lives should mean. It means we possess an essentially integrated sexuality, one that lets us sleep at night and stay within our commitments during the day. It means we carry responsibilities more than we ask others to carry us. It means we are essentially at ease, beyond the tumultuous restlessness of youth. Moreover, it means we have inside us now a certain solicitude, a healthy worry, an anxiety that is more about others than about ourselves. Of course, none of us achieves this perfectly, but maturity is defined by essentially achieving these things. We are mature when we are more altruistic than selfish.

Achieving this essential maturity is almost always concomitant with having a sense of being at home again. While we will struggle our whole lives to fully get ourselves together, the essential focus of our lives now shifts. We are now responsible adults, and this season of our lives will occupy us for the next fifty to sixty years, or perhaps for the rest of our lives. Moreover, this season has its own seasons. Our life as generative adults can be divided into two distinct seasons: *Early Generativity* and *Second Generativity*.

Early Generativity is the initial period of our maturity. This is the season in our lives when we marry, raise children, pay mortgages, work at various careers, work for our communities and churches, and are generally absorbed with all the necessary work, duty, and commitment that this asks of us. However, this time in our lives generally comes to a natural autumn—namely, to a time more for harvesting than for planting and nurturing. Sometime, normally in late midlife, we find our situation to be quite different. This is an invitation to a new season in our lives. Late midlife invites us to a Second Generativity, to a new kind of generativity and fruitfulness. Each of these seasons, as we will explore, has its own natural dictates.

EARLY GENERATIVITY

Early Generativity is generally a time when we find ourselves busy, habitually conscripted by duty, and mostly clear about what we should be doing. Our commitment to marriage, to children, to work, to our friends, to our communities, and to a vocation basically dictates what we need to do each day. This is not a season in our lives when we often wake up with the haunting question, Why should I get up this morning? Rather, an alarm clock rudely interrupts our sleep, and we get up unthinkingly because we do not need to think. The day is spelled out for us. A friend of mine shares a story where at a workshop on contemplative prayer, everyone was asking everyone else the question "What is your practice?" When asked that question, one woman, instead of sharing that her discipline was this or that particular contemplative practice, stated simply, "My practice is raising my kids!" That statement, with all it implies, can define what is asked of us in Early Generativity. These are years that are generally consumed with duty, busyness, pressures, worry about finances, and insecurities about our own measuring up.

SECOND GENERATIVITY

This second season of our lives as generative adults has a certain organic intelligence in it that naturally invites us into something new. At a certain point in life, circumstance lets you know that you are no longer a young woman or young man. The question now is, What are these ensuing years for? What do nature and God intend for you for these next twenty-five years? What do God and nature want of you now in terms of pouring out your creative energies? What are you called upon to give birth to now?

What is to be your post-menopausal baby, your "Isaac," your final gift to your loved ones and the world? What do love, marriage, duty, and commitment mean now when they have taken on a different modality?

It can be helpful to draw some perspectives from biology, which tells us that in the same way that huge biological changes take place in our bodies at puberty, so, too, do these changes take place later in life. For example, menopause, like puberty, causes changes in a woman's bodily structure and libidinal areas. This pushes her, whether she wants it or not, into a new phase of her life, one that asks for another initiation rite. Metaphorically, it pushes her out of "home" for a second time. That change also takes place in men, though in a less explicit way and in a way that, to their detriment, they can deny and resist somewhat longer.

Anthropology and archetypal psychology have some valuable insights to contribute to spirituality on the transition that is asked of us in late midlife. Our later years ask us to move beyond the "hungry child" and the "nurturing adult" to become the "blessing Elder." As well, they ask us to move from being a "wife" and a "mother" to being a "Sophia" and from being a "husband" and a "father" to being a "Magus."

What are our major struggles during these years? Psychologists speak of something they call midlife crisis—namely, a certain fatigue or acedia that can beset us and leave us vulnerable and tempted with the feeling that we did not make the right choices, that we want out of some of our present choices, and that we want another honeymoon. Of course not everyone undergoes this; but, if the literature of the mystics and some of the classical spiritual writers is to be believed, most everyone, during the long years of adulthood, will have to deal with some acedia: disillusionment, the temptation to revert to immaturity, boredom, resentment of duty, a certain joylessness bordering on anger, a

tendency to use busyness as an escape from dealing with relationships and inner work, a lack of awareness that this is a privileged
time in life, and a lack of gratitude for being healthy and in control. These struggles, John of the Cross says, are the trials that
beset us during both the early and late generative years of our
lives. These are the normal struggles on the long road of fidelity,
so we should not be surprised when we have to wrestle with them.
These are the dis-eases of an adult, and if we recognize them,
they can save us the pain of being crucified by a false romanticism
that would have us believe that on a long road there will not be
some dull, tiring stretches.

This is a time when we are freer from the restlessness of
our adolescence, a season when we can be home with pizza and a
movie on a Friday night. However, during this season, a different
kind of restlessness begins to creep in. Underneath a more tran-
quil surface and a quieter sexuality, we begin to sense an inchoate
disquiet that is beckoning us toward something we cannot yet
name and, against our attempts to ignore its voice, is letting us
know that we are going to have to leave home again. This is our
invitation to the third phase in our lives, *the struggle to give our
deaths away.*

THE THIRD SEASON: THE STRUGGLE
TO GIVE OUR DEATHS AWAY

In one of his last books, *Our Greatest Gift: A Meditation on Dying
and Caring,* Henri Nouwen says that at a certain point in our lives,
the question is no longer "What can I still do so that my life makes
a contribution?" Rather, it becomes "How can I live now so that
my death will be an optimal blessing to my family, the church,
and the world?" And the central question should not be "How
much time still remains?" but rather "How can I prepare now so

that my dying will be a new way for me to leave a warm, nurturing, and blessing spirit behind for those who have loved me and whom I have loved?"

For Nouwen, this is predicated on the fact that our lives belong not just to us but also to others. This is also true of our deaths. If we die with guilt, shame, anger, or bitterness, that will be part of what we leave to the world, and it will burden the lives of our family and friends. If we die unreconciled, in bitterness, most every memory we leave behind will cause unease, pain. And that will be our legacy. Conversely, if we die at peace, reconciled with our loved ones and the world, with a warm and grateful heart, then that warmth and love will be the spirit we leave behind, and most every memory of us will bring others warmth so that our dying in peace and reconciliation will then be our last gift—a wonderful, lasting one—to our loved ones. Giving our deaths away as a gift to our loved ones means that at some point in our lives, we need to stop focusing on our agenda and begin to focus on our obituary, on what kind of spirit we will leave behind.

T. S. Eliot once said, "To make an end is to make a beginning. The end is where we start from."

Hence, we begin.

TWO

|||||||||||||||||||||||||||||||

Some Anthropologies of Aging

The afternoon knows what the morning never suspected.

Don't accept the modern myths of aging.
You are not declining.
You are not fading away into uselessness.

JAMES HILLMAN: AGING AS AN
INTELLIGENCE INSIDE LIFE'S DNA

What did God and nature have in mind when they designed the aging process? Why is it that just when our mental prowess, human maturity, and emotional freedom are at their peak, the body begins to fall apart?

Faith, because it opens us to a perspective beyond our biological lives, sheds some light on these questions, though it doesn't always give us a language to grasp certain aspects of what is happening to us in the aging process. Sometimes a secular perspective can be helpful, and that is the case here.

James Hillman, in a brilliant book on aging entitled *The Force of Character,* takes up these questions. He answers with a metaphor: The best wines have to be aged in cracked old barrels. The last years of our lives are meant to mellow the soul, and most everything inside our biology conspires to ensure that this happens. The soul must be properly aged before it leaves. There's intelligence inside life, he asserts, that intends aging just as it intends growth in youth. It's a huge mistake to read the signs of aging as indications of dying rather than as initiations into another way of life. Each physical diminishment (from why we have to get up at night to go to the bathroom to why our skin sags and becomes dry) is designed to mature the soul. And each one does its work without our consent, relentlessly and ruthlessly.

The aging process, he asserts, eventually turns us all into monks—and that is indeed its plan. God is in on this conspiracy. Aging isn't always pleasant or easy, but there's a rhyme and reason to the process. Aging deliteralizes biology. The soul finally gets to trump the body and rise to the fore. "We can then imagine aging as a transformation in beauty as much as in biology," writes Hillman. "The old are like images on display that transpose biological life into imagination, into art. The old become strikingly memorable, ancestral representations, characters in the play of civilization, each a unique, irreplaceable figure of value. Aging: an art form?"

As we age, our task is not productivity but reflection, not utility but character. In Hillman's words, "Earlier years must focus on getting things done, while later years consider what was done and how." The former is a function of generativity; we are meant to give our lives away. The latter is a function of dying; we are also meant to give our deaths away.

And the aging process raises a second series of questions: What value do the elderly have once their productive years are over? Indeed, the same question might be asked of anyone who cannot be useful and productive in a practical sense: What is the value of someone living with Alzheimer's? What is the value of people continuing to live in palliative care when there is no chance of recovery or improvement and they have already slipped away from us mentally? What is the value of the life of a person who is so mentally or physically challenged that by normal standards he or she cannot contribute anything?

Again, Hillman's insights are a valuable supplement to the perspectives offered us through faith. For Hillman, what aging and disability bring into our lives is character, and not just our own: They give character to others. Thus, he writes,

> Productivity is too narrow a measure of usefulness, disability too cramping a notion of helplessness. An older woman may be helpful simply as a figure valued for her character. Like a stone at the bottom of a riverbed, she may do nothing but stay still and hold her ground, but the river has to take her into account and alter its flow because of her. An older man by sheer presence plays his part as a character in the drama of the family and the neighborhood. He has to be considered, and patterns adjusted simply because he is there. His character brings particular qualities to every scene, adds to their intricacy and depth by representing the past and the dead. When all the elderly are removed to retirement communities, the river flows more smoothly back home. No disruptive rocks. Less character, too.

We as a culture do everything we can to deny, delay, and disguise aging. We put our elders in separate homes, tucked away from mainstream life—no disruptive rocks for us to deal with.

We as a culture are also beginning to talk more and more about euthanasia, defining value purely by utility. If Hillman is right, and he is, then we are paying a high price for this. Independent of all moral considerations (which do have an impact here), we have less character and less color.

Finally, Hillman feels that it is important to decouple aging from death and instead link it to character and value. He puts it this way: "'Old' is present in degrees in many phenomena whose character we admire, like old ships, old shacks, old photographs; here, 'old' refers neither to something grown into after middle age nor to something en route to death." God and nature had something positive and generative in mind when they inserted aging into the natural human cycle. Aging has its own specific purpose and intent and is not simply the debilitating last road that takes us toward death. Aging is intended to mellow the soul and bring out character.

A LESSON FROM HINDU ANTHROPOLOGY

Hinduism is perhaps the oldest religion in the world today, with well over one billion followers. It has a wonderfully developed anthropology and spirituality of aging. It sees *four* stages to our lives and suggests a very specific spirituality for each stage. In its view, these are the four essential stages in life: *Student, House-holder, Forest Dweller,* and *Sannyasin.*

First, we begin life as children; for Hindus, this is not yet marked off as a particular stage in life. As a child, one is living with his parents or other guardians and is, in effect, being equipped with the tools for life: language, manners, faith, and the skills to take care of himself. This is considered not a stage in life but more simply a preparation for one's journey into life.

The first marked stage of life in Hinduism is that of a *Stu-*

dent. Traditionally this begins with a rite of initiation somewhere between the ages of eight and twelve, and traditionally this stage lasts for twelve years. One's primary responsibility during these years is to learn, particularly to soak up the wisdom of one's elders and traditions. This is seen as an apprenticeship that prepares a person for the responsibilities of adulthood, marriage, parenting, supporting a family, religious and civic duties, and being an elder who can mentor others.

The second stage, which Hindus term being a *Householder,* begins with marriage. This inserts a person into the center of life and asks that her attention 'now be focused on three things: family, vocation, and community. This will be the focus of her life until late midlife, when there will be a natural decline in attachment to the duties that flow from family, vocation, and community. The pleasure derived from sex and career success will shift in meaning, begin to pale, and leave her grasping for new meaning, which will then beckon her to the next stage in life. However, not everyone goes there. Many choose to simply continue to cling to the lives they have lived until now, not making any changes unless forced to by health or circumstance. But some meet this stage of their lives proactively and voluntarily set out toward something new, a time in "the forest."

A person in this third stage is called a *Forest Dweller.* Classically, one enters it when he becomes a grandparent. His child-raising duties are now done, as are his duties to society; his responsibilities are now primarily to himself. At this stage in life, a person leaves his occupation, family, and civic duties behind, as well as his youthful hopes and dreams. Practically, the way he does this is by physically leaving his family (husbands and wives might do this together) and setting out on a journey of discovery, archetypally imaged as going off into the deep forest to take instructions from the elders who dwell there. In reality, this might mean anything from living in a monastery for a time; to spending some time in solitude, study, and prayer; to apprenticing himself as a disciple to some holy person or wisdom figure; to going on an extended pilgrimage.

However, this was always understood as being a temporary period of life, a time of preparation for the final stage, a time of transition when a person tries to discern and create a vision of what his final stage of life is supposed to be. This is his retirement, but not yet the final stage of his life. This is a school to prepare him for what he believes should, ideally, be the last stage of his life: being a holy beggar.

In the fourth and final stage of life in Hinduism, one becomes a *Sannyasin,* a *Holy Beggar.* Archetypally, this was imaged as becoming a saint who is a beggar—someone who, while deep in compassion, no longer has any ties to this world. She has no home, no practical occupation, no belongings, no means of support, no social status or social pretensions of any kind. She is simply a holy tramp, a beggar, but someone who incarnates holiness and can be turned to for counsel or simply just touched for grace. Archetypally, the *Sannyasin* sits without pride, helpless, supported only by a begging bowl, indifferent to life or death, already radiating eternity.

Comparing the stages of life in Hinduism to how we understand those stages in our secular world and within Christian spirituality, we do not see a lot of difference, except for one salient point: the stage Hindus call *Forest Dwelling.* Hinduism has this transition stage (which we lack) between retiring from being a *Householder* (our concept of retirement) and living out one's last years. Their understanding offers something Christian spirituality does not—namely, an intermediate, transition stage in which one spends some months or years proactively studying, praying, being mentored, and doing inner work to both ready his soul and constellate a vision of what his final years might mean in terms of a new generativity; or, perhaps more radically, this stage gives one the vision and inner resources to become some kind of "holy beggar."

GERMAINE GREER: THE STAGES OF A WOMAN'S LIFE

Among her many books, the colorful Australian writer Germaine Greer wrote one entitled *The Change: Women, Ageing and the Menopause.* While this is a book about female menopause, it throws some rich light on the issue of aging for everyone, both women and men.

Greer sees six stages in a woman's life, which she gives these names:

1. Infancy/Childhood
2. Adolescence/Nubility
3. Wifehood
4. Motherhood
5. Menopause/Transition
6. Crone/Elder

A woman begins her life as an *Infant* and as a *Child.* For Greer, as for Hinduism, this is essentially a time of learning, of preparing, of acquiring the manners and skills to meet adolescence, ready for its challenges. At this stage, there is not much of a distinction between how girls are treated and how they think of themselves and how boys are raised and think of themselves, except that most little girls learn early on that what is really important for them is that they be pretty, that they have a body that is admired. Little girls, early on, breathe in an air that tells them they will be valued by society more for their biology than for their soul.

This is then reinforced powerfully in the second stage of a woman's life, *Adolescence/Nubility*. During this period of her life, there is fierce pressure from the culture, the fashion industry, the media, and her peers—and a certain ideal of femininity—to look good; she receives a clear message that her body is ultimately what defines her and gives her value. And at this point in her life, she often receives unwelcome attention from men. They whistle at her from across the street, make unwelcome passes at her, and sometimes sexually harass her. There are few women who have not experienced sexual harassment in this and the next period of their lives. And all this reinforces the sense inside them that they are seen and valued basically for biology rather than for their minds and souls.

From *Adolescence/Nubility,* the woman (at least in the majority of cases) moves on to what Greer calls *Wifehood.* This changes things somewhat in that a good marriage can help the woman recover a healthier sense of her person, soul, and value. Sometimes entry into a career can also help her see that she is more than just an attractive body. But she is still aware, consciously or unconsciously, that what the world wants from her is an attractive body.

Then she enters the stage of *Motherhood.* She gives birth to children, the most marvelous of all biological miracles. And in this stage, she experiences the biological earthiness of nursing babies, toilet training toddlers, feeding children, wiping their faces, putting bandages on their wounds, and tending to their every need. Motherhood is an experience that can fundamentally change how a woman understands purpose and meaning so that, for her, it is not so important anymore that she have the perfect body, though that old pressure never fully dies. However, as Greer points out, as a mother, she is still valued for her biology, and the danger is that she will continue to inhale that in terms of her self-understanding. Be that as it may, her experience of motherhood can be enough to give her meaning and purpose for many years, until nature intervenes with menopause.

Menopause, akin to what puberty did decades earlier, fundamentally reorients a woman. Metaphorically, it drives her out of home again, at least from what she for many years considered "home." Major biological changes trigger concomitant emotional and psychological changes and move the woman into a certain liminal space—namely, a situation in which something fundamental in her former way of life (and concept of herself) is over and she is staring at a new horizon with no option of returning to the old. For Greer, this is a pivotal moment in a woman's life and catches many women unprepared. Up until midlife, a woman has unconsciously taken so much of her identity and meaning from her biology, and that biology is now betraying her. From menopause onward, the woman will need to establish a purpose and meaning for herself that is not based on her biology.

In Greer's view, often neither the woman nor society is prepared for this shift. For society, the woman now becomes invisible. This invisibility has a double aspect. Society no longer has an honored place for her, and she, who as a young girl was too visible and received so much unwelcome attention, now finds herself invisible as she sits at a table in a restaurant wondering why the waiter never seems to notice her. That invisibility is seen in literature and the arts. For instance, Greer points out that in literature and movies, there are precious few female heroines older than fifty. Society wants young women with perfect bodies as its heroines. Hence, this can be a time of cruel adjustment for women. Having been valued for their biology for many years and given a certain place in society because of it, women can be disoriented by the fact that society is no longer interested in them. Interestingly, Greer, who was schooled by nuns, points out that nuns (and other women) who have not given themselves to marriage and children but who made a commitment in their early adult years to a vocation of wider service often do not experience the same kind of disorientation at menopause; through their vows or other commitments, they had already defined themselves as a mentor and a wisdom figure, a Sophia, rather than as someone's wife and mother.

So, to what is this liminal space called menopause inviting a woman? It is inviting her into the final stage of a woman's life, that of being a *Crone,* an *Elder.* Biblically and archetypally, we might call this becoming a Sophia. The task in life now is no longer to take pains to look particularly pretty, to be someone's spouse, or to give birth to or nurture children. The task of a Sophia, a *Crone* and an *Elder,* is to initiate energy, to teach, to counsel, to heal, to console, and to speak the "sacred" words and perform the healing rituals for each occasion. While the woman remains someone's wife and someone's mother, that is no longer her generative purpose nor the core of her identity. Sophia is nobody's wife and nobody's mother; she is everyone's counselor.

While teaching their own specific lessons vis-à-vis the struggles of women at a particular time in their lives, these stages of life, Greer proposes, complement how Christian spirituality understands both the psychological and spiritual struggles in the second half of life. Like Christian spirituality, these stages highlight the difference between early generativity in the first half of life and second generativity in the second half of life. *Wifehood* and *Motherhood* are one kind of generativity; becoming an *Elder* and being a Sophia is another kind. In biblical imagery, Sophia is the aged Sarah, giving birth to a child post-menopause.

A final word on Greer's insights: This is a book about a woman's stages of life and how a second puberty, menopause, invites and pushes women into a new generativity; it does not stretch things explicitly regarding how this might apply to men. Men do not undergo menopause in an biological fashion like women do, but they do undergo (in a less clearly pronounced way) the same changes, biologically and psychologically, with the same meaning and the same invitation. Men, of course, can go into denial about these changes and, with the aid of modern medicines, extend their biological generative potentials, but that only delays their development. Nature and God have the same designs for men, and midlife and beyond bring changes in a man's body that are an invitation to a post-menopausal generativity.

RICHARD ROHR: A RADICALLY SUCCINCT ANTHROPOLOGY OF AGING

Roman Catholic spiritual writer Richard Rohr offers a wonderfully succinct but far-reaching anthropology and spirituality of aging. For Rohr, even though we may all reach the second half of life through different journeys, at a certain point, somewhere between the ages of fifty and seventy, we all stand on exactly the same plane, looking at exactly the same options for our future. Then, regardless of how we got there, we all have the same *three* options, and only those options: We can age into a *"pathetic old fool"*; we can age into an *"angry old fool"*; or we can age into a *"holy old fool."* Notice what is common among the three: Someday we will all be old fools. We will be marginalized by society, struggle with an aging body that is breaking down, and be conscious of the fact that we are no longer needed as we once were. We all will eventually be old fools, but we get to choose what kind of fool we will be: pathetic, angry, or holy.

The word "pathetic" comes from the Greek word *pathos,* meaning "painful, sad." A *pathetic old fool* is someone who, while old, has never accepted his age and is trying, by every means possible, to somehow still be young, whether this means undergoing multiple cosmetic surgeries, buying a new sports car at age seventy-five, taking pills to extend his sexual abilities, or leaving his partner for someone younger. There is something sad and futile in these efforts. However, this needs some nuance. Indeed, there is nothing wrong with trying to stay young, healthy, and physically attractive as we age. One of the first signs of depression is when one ceases to care about his vigor, health, and attractiveness. A healthy person will try to stay vigorous and physically attractive as long as possible, but a healthy person will also accept his age and the fact that it is calling him to something deeper than merely appearing still young and attractive. The pathos and sadness enter when one is not living inside his own skin but is denying one kind of life and striving restlessly to live with the spirit of another kind of life. When one's actual life and one's spirit are not in sync, there is pathos.

The second option is to become an *angry old fool.* This, it seems, is the more popular option. All too common is the senior citizen who is angry and bitter. At issue here is not someone denying one's age and trying to stay young at all costs. Aging and its diminishment are accepted but at a price: anger, bitterness about being in this state and about how one's life has turned out. Psychologists tell us that this happens not because we grow angry when we get old but rather that when we grow old, all the old angers we have stored up through the years break through the fragile dikes that had been containing them. It is never, we are told, a question of getting angry when we are old, but perennially the issue of an angry person growing old. This is perhaps the major psychological and spiritual danger we face in our lives: giv-

ing in to more and more anger as we age and leaving this world
with a bitter heart.

However, Rohr says there is a third option: We can become a
holy old fool. A holy old fool is someone just as marginalized by
age, health, and society as everyone else but who has made peace
with that. Being holy here does not necessarily refer to anything
particularly spiritual, religious, pious, or even outstandingly altruistic. A holy old fool does not need to look like John the Bap-
tist, Mother Teresa, or a Hindu *sannyasin.* She simply needs to
look like someone who is at peace inside her own skin and, because of that, emits a certain peace, order, and joy to those around
her. A holy old fool is someone who has accepted the debilitation
and marginalization that comes with age; has sufficiently grieved
her wounds, her disappointments, and the injustices she experienced in her life; and has forgiven everything and everybody, including herself and God. A holy old fool is okay with being old
and is okay with the hand life has dealt her.

Rohr has another fruitful image, an image taken from the
Book of Job, to describe how we might view aging and dying. In
a very poignant phrase, Job says, "Naked I came from my mother's womb, and naked shall I return." For Rohr, this represents
the two halves of life. We emerge from our mother's womb
naked—not just that we are not physically clothed but naked in
every sense. We are born without a name, a language, a self-image,
any possessions of our own, and even an ego. We spend the first
half of our lives metaphorically covering that nakedness—that is,
accumulating: We are given a name, learn to speak, and acquire
various diplomas, certificates of achievement, friends, possessions
of all kinds, a reputation, and a strong ego. That is very much
what consumes us during the first half of our lives: We accumu-
late.

The second half of life (which for Rohr does not begin until later in midlife) is about shedding, about metaphorically leaving most of that clothing behind and moving again toward nakedness. And, for Rohr, the key thing we need to keep shedding and shedding is the ego we have acquired.

For Rohr, in both his notions of aging, the major psychological and spiritual task is one of letting go, of acceptance, of surrender. Like Jesus on the cross, ultimately we need to bow our heads and give over our spirits.

ALICE MILLER: AGING AND THE DRAMA OF THE GIFTED CHILD

A generation ago, Polish Swiss psychologist Alice Miller wrote a famous book entitled *The Drama of the Gifted Child.* Among the many insights she shares, one sheds some very helpful light on the struggles we face in aging.

She describes something she calls the drama of the gifted child. What is this drama? For Miller, the gifted child is not necessarily the child born with the highest intelligence quotient or with some extraordinary artistic or athletic talent. For her, the gifted child is the extraordinarily sensitive child, the child who right from day one feels things deeply and responds with a concomitant sensitivity. Such a person, she says, will experience a lot of hurt in his life; but, being sensitive to the feelings of others, he will bury that hurt inside himself rather than lash out at others when they hurt him. And he will carry that hurt into midlife, mostly silently and stoically, as if he has not been hurt. Then, for reasons of every sort, the dikes will give way and all that stored-up hurt will break through. As a friend of mine is fond of saying, when you reach the age of forty, you realize that what you suspected all along is true: Your mother did love your sister more than she loved you! That realization of hurt and unfairness triggers the drama of the gifted child—that is, what to do with all the hurts inside, given that they are real, given that they are deeply affecting who the person is and how he loves, and given his over-sensitivity in dealing with them.

So, how can the gifted child resolve this drama? For Miller, one resolves this drama through grieving. As she puts it, the major task of midlife and beyond is to grieve until the roots of your foundations shake. Your wounds are real, and denial and stoicism are no longer your friends. Staying with them will turn you bitter. Your mother did love your sister more than you, and there is nothing you can do to change that; but you can grieve it, and that can soften the hardness inside you. And once the hardness is gone, you will be able to forgive your mother, your sister, and, not least, yourself for believing all these years that you were not worthy of your mother's love.

For Alice Miller, the major—perhaps sole—psychological and spiritual task of midlife and beyond is grieving so as to come to forgiveness.

DAVID BROOKS: AGING AND THE INVITATION TO SCALE THE SECOND MOUNTAIN

New York Times columnist David Brooks, in his book *The Second Mountain: The Quest for a Moral Life,* using his own life's story and drawing upon both Christianity and Judaism, offers some valuable insights toward an anthropology and spirituality for aging. Indeed, his term "the second mountain" is quite synony-mous with what spirituality authors such as Richard Rohr call "the second half of life." In this book, Brooks presents his vision for the second half of life and suggests a road map on how to get there.

For Brooks, most of us make four major commitments over

the course of our lives: We commit to a vocation, to a spouse and family, to a philosophy or a faith, and to a community. Each of these requires certain things from us: dedication, an investment of time and effort, a willingness to close off other options, and a certain leap of faith. But how we live this out can vary greatly between the first half of our lives (climbing the "first mountain") and the second half (scaling the "second mountain").

Here is how he contrasts the two: The first mountain, which is our journey into midlife and maturity, is often focused on exhibiting individualism, searching for personal happiness, achieving independence and autonomy, taking charge, developing a career, accomplishing goals, promoting self-interest, buying and selling, taking care of ourselves, keeping our options open, and finding ourselves. In contrast, the second mountain, which is the task of midlife and beyond, needs to be focused on finding meaning, experiencing moral joy, being interdependent, developing relationships, listening, re-enchanting our perception of things, doing acts of love that take us beyond self-interest, loving others, making commitments and keeping them, and giving ourselves away.

To do this, Brooks suggests, requires a major motivational shift, a walking away from a former way of life, moral reflection, a greater trust and vulnerability, and a desire to become responsible in love-drenched accountability. Also, the vision and capacity to make this shift is normally predicated on having a proper sense of vocation in life.

Carl Jung once defined a vocation this way: "an irrational factor that destines a man to emancipate himself from the herd and from its well-worn paths." Frederick Buechner, the famed preacher, submits that a vocation is "where . . . your deep gladness meets the world's deep hunger." Brooks quotes them both and then adds that a vocation is not something we choose but rather something that chooses us. When we sense it as a possibility in our lives, we also sense that we do not have a choice but can only ask ourselves, What is my responsibility here? It is not a matter of what we expect from life but rather what life expects from us. Moreover, for Brooks, once we have a sense of vocation, it becomes unthinkable to turn away, and we sense that we would be morally culpable if we did. He quotes William Wordsworth in support of this:

> *My heart was full; I made no vows, but vows*
> *Were then made for me; bond unknown to me*
> *Was given, that I should be, else sinning greatly.*

Brooks then suggests that any number of things can help awaken our souls to their vocation: music, drama, art, friendship, children, beauty, and, paradoxically, injustice. To this he adds two further observations: first, that we usually see and understand all this clearly only when we are older and looking back on our lives and our choices; and, second, that while the summons to a vocation is a holy thing, something mystical, the way we actually end up living it is often messy and confusing and generally does not feel holy at all.

Things can awaken us to our vocation, but how do we know our vocation? The answer generally does not come in an overpowering flash of insight, or in some extraordinary movement of heart, or even in a strong attraction to a certain way of life. The answer usually comes as a hook in our conscience, as something being asked of us, as something we cannot morally turn away from, and as something we might initially resist. A vocation chooses us and makes the commitments for us—and those commitments put us at that place in the world where we are best placed to serve others and to find happiness.

As we age and move into the second half of our lives, Brooks suggests there are three paths for growth that we might take as a road map:

1. From *suffering* to *wisdom* to *service*

2. From *dying to the old self,* to *cleansing in the emptiness,* to *resurrecting in the new*

3. From *the agony of the valley,* to *the purgation in the desert,* to *the insight on the mountaintop*

And all this, he says, will leave us radiating a "bright sadness," which is what depth of soul looks like on the surface.

KATHLEEN DOWLING SINGH: THE AGING AND DYING PROCESS AS CALIBRATED TO BRING US INTO THE REALM OF SPIRIT

Kathleen Dowling Singh was a hospice worker, psychotherapist, and influential spiritual writer. She was known and deeply respected among those who work in the area of spirituality on the strength of three major books: *The Grace in Living, The Grace in Aging,* and *The Grace in Dying.* It is interesting to note that she worked backward in writing this trilogy, beginning with dying, moving on to aging, and finally offering a reflection on living. She wrote in this order because her grounding insights were taken from her experience as a hospice worker attending to terminally ill patients. What she learned from being with and observing the dying taught her a lot about what it means to age and, ultimately, what it means to live. Her books highlight the deep grace that is inherent in each of these stages in our lives: living, aging, dying.

For our purposes, I will focus on the insights from her book *The Grace in Dying.* Outside of Scripture and some classical mys-

tics, you will be hard-pressed to find as deep a spiritual understanding of what God and nature intend in the process we go
through in aging and dying. Singh encapsulates her thesis that
the process of aging and dying is exquisitely calibrated to bring us
into the realm of spirit. There is a wisdom in the aging and dying
process. Here is what it is designed to do.

Throughout our lives, our self-consciousness radically limits
our awareness, effectively closing off much of the realm of spirit.
But that is not how we were born. As babies, we were wonderfully open and aware—except, lacking self-consciousness and
ego, we were not aware of what we were aware. A baby is lumi-
nous, but a baby can't think. In order to think, it needs to form an
ego and become self-aware. According to Singh, the formation of
that ego, the condition for self-awareness, is predicated on our
making four massive mental contractions, each of which closes
off some of our awareness of the world of spirit.

We form our egos this way: First, early in a baby's life, the
baby makes *a distinction between what is self and what is other.* That
is the first major contraction. Soon afterward, the baby makes *a
distinction between living and nonliving*—a puppy is alive; a stone
is not. Sometime after that, the baby makes *a distinction between
mind and body*—a body is solid and physical in a way that the
mind is not. Finally, early on in our lives, we make *a distinction
between what we can face inside ourselves and what is too overwhelming to face.* We separate our own luminosity and complexity from
our conscious awareness, forming what is often called our *shadow.*
Each of these movements effectively shuts off whole realms of
reality from our awareness. By doing that, Singh says, we create
our fear of death.

Now—and this is Singh's pregnant insight—the process of
aging and dying effectively breaks down these contractions in reverse order of how we formed them, and, with each breakdown,

we become more aware again of a wider realm of reality, particularly the realm of spirit. And this culminates in the last moments or seconds before our deaths, in an experience of ecstasy, observable in many terminal patients as they die. As the last contraction that formed our ego is broken, spirit breaks through and we move into ecstasy. As a hospice worker, Singh claims to have seen this many times in her patients.

Elisabeth Kübler-Ross, in *On Death and Dying*—which has now essentially become the canon by how we understand the stages of dying—suggests that someone diagnosed with a terminal disease will go through *five* stages before her death: *denial, anger, bargaining, depression, acceptance.* Singh would agree, except that she would add three further stages: *a fall into darkness that verges on despair, a resignation that dwarfs initial acceptance,* and *a breaking in of ecstasy.* She points out that Jesus went through those exact stages on the cross: a cry of abandonment that sounds like despair, the handing over of his spirit, and the ecstasy that was given him in his death.

Singh's theory on the intent of the aging and dying process is both insightful and consoling. The process of aging and dying will do for us what a deep life of prayer and selflessness was meant to do for us—namely, break our selfishness and open us to the realm of spirit.

The process of aging and dying has clear intent: God will get us, one way or the other.

THREE
||||||||||||||||||||||||||||||||||

The Challenge in Aging
From Achievement to Fruitfulness

The ultimate question that any of us, or any art, can ask is this: "How may I die generously?"

AGING AS MELLOWING OUR SOULS
THROUGH A SERIES OF TRANSITIONS

The human aging process is designed to mellow the soul, analogous to how the best wines are aged in cracked old barrels. As we age, our bodies become, figuratively and literally, cracked old barrels in which our souls are given a unique opportunity to mellow. But what inside a soul needs to be mellowed? What makes for hardness of soul? For immaturity of soul? For greenness? For sourness?

Our bodies begin more and more to betray us as we grow older, and we naturally feel less secure in their old ways and feel pressure to change and let go of some things, even at the cost of great pain to ourselves. As we sense the mortality of the body, we realize that we must make some changes or we will leave this world in an unhappy state and leave behind a less than blessing spirit. Consciously or subconsciously, we realize that we are being asked to undergo a life-altering transformation and that this will be a very painful, purgative process.

What is this transformation asking of us? The transformation might be summarized in these *seven* movements:

1. From *resentment* to *gratitude*

2. From *bitterness* to *forgiveness*

3. From *imagination* to *faith*

4. From *wishful thinking and natural optimism* to *hope*

5. From *sophistication* to *childlikeness*

6. From *control* to *surrender*

7. From *achievement* to *fruitfulness*

From Resentment to Gratitude

When he was in his eighties, the novelist Morris West wrote a short, though remarkable, memoir recounting many of his struggles during his life and how he eventually made peace with all that was wounded inside him. Writing as an old man still bearing the scars of some bitter fires he has been through, he offers us some advice. When you reach a certain age, he says, there should be only three phrases left in your vocabulary: *Thank you, Thank you,* and *Thank you.* If we reach our autumn years and these are not the dominant three phrases in our vocabulary, then we still have some major inner work to do.

Indeed, the capacity to say thank you, to be grateful, is the ultimate virtue underlying all other virtues, including love. Unless it is fueled by gratitude, anything that poses as love or altruism will be in some way self-serving and manipulative. It is not incidental that when Jesus leaves us the Eucharist and asks us to perpetuate it until the end of time, he does not simply say, "Receive this, break it among yourselves, and share it." He inserts a critical phrase: Receive, *Give thanks,* Break, and Share. Before we can truly share anything in love, we need first to give thanks; otherwise, our love will have a false coloring. Even while doing the right thing, it will be done for some of the wrong reasons.

All of us come to adulthood and to our autumn years carrying deep wounds that, unless they are properly grieved and opened to grace and healing, will leave us resentful and bitter. And ideally that is not how we want to live out our last years and say goodbye to our loved ones and our world. We want to die with a warm, grateful heart.

The aging and dying process is designed to help us move from resentment to gratitude.

From Bitterness to Forgiveness

In 2007, William Young wrote a novel, *The Shack,* that captured the popular imagination, even though it did not always endear itself to churches. This is its storyline: A man is on a trip with his daughter when she is kidnapped and murdered. In the days and weeks after, in his bitterness, he continually nurses angry, vengeful thoughts. A few years after her murder, he receives a letter inviting him to a meeting in the shack where the bloodied clothing of his murdered daughter was found. He sets out, angry, armed, expecting to confront the murderer, but instead he meets God. He has long conversations with God, but God's ultimate message to him is that he has to forgive his daughter's murderer and that nothing else is as strong a spiritual imperative as forgiveness. Forgiving others is a nonnegotiable prerequisite to entering heaven, even if the one you are asked to forgive murdered your daughter.

Some churches reacted to the book, concerned it made it sound as though forgiveness of others is the sole requirement for entering heaven. What about keeping the commandments? What about churchgoing? Aren't these important? Admittedly, those are valid concerns, but at the end of the day, William Young is right. Forgiving others is the ultimate prerequisite to taking a seat at the heavenly banquet table. Jesus says so. After teaching us the Lord's Prayer (which includes the petition "Forgive us our debts, as we also have forgiven our debtors"), he warns us that if we do not forgive one another, God will not forgive us. Why not? Why will God not forgive our sins if we do not forgive others?

The issue is not God's willingness or unwillingness. The issue is rather harmony at God's table. In simple terms, the table of God is open to everyone who is willing to sit down with everyone. God does not have separate tables for those who cannot sit down with one another. Hence, if we cannot forgive another, how can we be at God's table with him? In the end, we can slim down our spiritual vocabulary to very few words, but prominent among those words is "forgiveness."

This is a challenge, perhaps the ultimate challenge for all of us. Life can be brutally unfair, and we can be sinfully unfaithful. It is hard to forgive others, and it is perhaps even harder to forgive ourselves. Hence, sometime before we die, we need to forgive—forgive those who wounded or failed us, forgive ourselves for our own failures, and then forgive God because life is sometimes unfair. We need to do this so that we do not die angry, bitter people. That is the final challenge of our lives.

Ira Byock, a physician and author who works in palliative care, wrote a series of books about what ideally should happen during the process of aging and dying. He summarizes it all in a short series of phrases—namely, *the four things that matter most.* The four things that are most important to say on our deathbed (if we have not said them with sufficient heart before) are *"Please forgive me," "I forgive you," "Thank you,"* and *"I love you."*

However, as we know from bitter experience, forgiveness is not something we can do simply by flipping some internal emotional and spiritual switch. It is a process, often a lifelong one. The wounds to our souls, like the wounds to our bodies, take time—sometimes a lifetime—to heal. That is why, within the Judeo-Christian spirituality of Sabbath, there is an embedded wisdom and a certain divine permission concerning the process of moving toward forgiveness.

The theology and spirituality of Sabbath teach us that God created the world in six days and then rested on the seventh day, the Sabbath. Moreover, not only did God rest on the Sabbath, but God also declared this a day of rest for everyone forever, and with that God set up a certain rhythm for our lives. That rhythm is supposed to work this way:

- We work for six days and then rest for one day.
- We work for seven years and then rest for one year (a sabbatical).
- We work for seven times seven years (forty-nine years) and then have jubilee, where the world itself goes on sabbatical.
- We work for a lifetime and then enjoy an eternity of sabbatical.

Moreover, that rhythm is also the rhythm for how we need to forgive others:

- We can hold a mini grudge for seven days, but then we need to give it up.
- We can hold a major grudge for seven years, but then we need to give it up. (The statute of limitations is based on this.)
- We can hold a massive soul-searing grudge for forty-nine years, but then we need to give it up.
- We can hold a wound that destroyed our life until our deathbed, but then we need to give it up.

The intent of the aging and dying process is to help us let go of the bitterness that has constellated inside us through the years so that during our last years and our last moments, we will be saying the four things that matter most.

From Imagination to Faith

In all true religions, the first thing taught about God is that God is ineffable. That means that because God is infinite, God cannot be captured in any concept, thought, or imaginative construct. God can be known, but God cannot be thought. However, we are creatures of thought, of imagination, of concepts; hence, we are always creating for ourselves imaginative images of God. And these are good and helpful for a while. When we are young in faith, we need images, pictures, imaginative constructs. A God who cannot be captured in thought can easily cease to exist for us.

However, necessary as these imaginative pictures of God are in our early religious development, they are still, in the end, just that: pictures, not the reality. A mature faith at some point has to move beyond images, pictures, and notions and come face-to-face with the reality behind those pictures. Paradoxically, this can feel like a loss of faith (agnosticism) or even like atheism. But when our images of God disappear, what is left? The reality. But the reality doesn't feel as real as the images. Why?

A mother fish at the bottom of the ocean is approached by baby fish who say to her, "Mother, what is water? Show us water!" The irony is that they are immersed in water, and because of that they cannot have a concept of water. So, let's take this imaginative story a little further. The mother decides to give them a concept of water. She sets up a PowerPoint projector and begins to show them slides of water: Niagara Falls, a running tap, the ocean waves rolling, kids splashing in a pool, a dolphin diving out of the ocean. Initially, the baby fish will be intrigued; these pictures have given them a concept of water. But these are pictures, not water. Because of this, after a sufficient time, the mother fish will turn off the projector and tell them simply, "Those were pictures of water, not water; but now you have some notion of water, so just sit in it, swim in it, and let it flow through you!" Ironically, the water they are immersed in will not seem real to them. With the projector turned off, no longer showing the pictures of water, they can now easily become agnostic about their belief in water.

That is the difference between imagination and faith. Imagination provides us with pictures, with PowerPoint slides of God, but none of these images are God. They are icons at best, idols at worst. This is true even of our Scriptures. The Bible is not God but merely a normative PowerPoint presentation about God. Mystical literature, from Scripture down through the classical mystics, tells us that faith is believing in something we cannot conceptualize or picture. But we do not move there easily; we naturally cling to our images.

The aging and dying process is one of the ways that God (conspiring with nature) moves us from imagination to faith. As we age, our old securities break down; among these are our imaginative ideas about God. Mystics call this breakdown of our for-

mer ways of knowing God "a dark night of the soul" and assure
us that it is disillusioning and painful but also radically purifying.

From Wishful Thinking and Natural Optimism to Hope

We tend to misunderstand hope, confusing it with wishful thinking and temperamental optimism. It is neither. For instance,
someone will say, "I hope I win the lottery." You can only wish to
win the lottery. Your wish is not based upon anything other than
your own desire and longing, and this has no real bearing on reality. Hope is grounded in reality. The same holds true of natural
optimism. Frequently we hear someone say, "I'm a hopeful person; I always see the bright side of things!" That can make for a
pleasant temperament, but it does not make for hope. Someone
can be an optimist and lack hope, just as someone can be a pessi-
mist and be full of hope. So, what, exactly, is hope?

The scientist, philosopher, and mystic Pierre Teilhard de
Chardin (1881–1955) was once challenged while giving a presentation. In his presentation, he brought together the scientific theory of evolution with his vision of faith, a vision in which history
is seen to culminate in a community of life, among all creatures,
such as is taught in the Christian Scriptures. He was challenged
with this question: "Suppose we blow up the world with a nuclear
bomb; what happens then?" Teilhard answered in words to this
effect: If we blow up the world with a nuclear bomb, that would
be a setback of millions of years. But the vision I am affirming
here will come to fruition, not because I wish it, but because God
promised it, and in the resurrection of Jesus, God showed that
God has the power to deliver on that promise.

That, for a Christian, is the definition of hope. Hope is not
based on wishful thinking or an optimistic look at the situation in
the world. It is based on God's promise and God's power, and our
trust in both that promise and that power is predicated on belief

in the resurrection of Jesus. As Saint Paul says, if the resurrection did not happen, then we are the most deluded of all people and there is no basis for hope. However, if we believe in the resurrection, we have an unshakable basis for hope that is based in reality.

During the height of the struggle against apartheid in South Africa, the military would sometimes try to intimidate Archbishop Desmond Tutu while he was preaching. Tutu would begin a sermon, and the military would enter the church and line up in the side aisles. Tutu would smile at them and say, "I'm glad that you came to join the winning side. We have already won!" But he was not talking about apartheid; he was talking about a much bigger victory, the resurrection of Jesus, which (if believed) assures us that the end of our story has already been written and that it is a happy ending, one of complete vindication and triumph.

The Swiss theologian Hans Urs von Balthasar (1905–1988) offers us this image: Imagine you are an actor in a five-act play. You are scripted to triumph in the end. However, in the four acts leading up to your triumph and vindication, you are subject to every kind of humiliation and seemingly hopeless situation. As an actor, you already know the ending, and so you have that perspective whenever things seem hopeless. In the famous words of the mystic Julian of Norwich (1342–1416), you know that in the end "all shall be well, and all shall be well, and all manner of thing shall be well." The ending to our story is already written, and our hope for that ending is not mere wishful thinking, nor is it grounded on the fact that for a season or so the world news has looked more hopeful. It is grounded on God's promise and God's power to deliver on that promise.

One last image: Some years ago, I attended a presentation given by a French Canadian Oblate missionary, Pierre Olivier Tremblay. As part of introducing his reflection, he shared this:

I work as a chaplain on a university campus. I minister with young women and men in their late teens and early twenties. They are wonderfully full of life, energy, and dreams, *but they have no hope because they don't have a meta-narrative.* They only have their own individual story, and their lives go up and down more or less exclusively on the basis of what is happening to them on a given day. If things are going well in terms of their significant relationships, their friendships, their health, and their studies, they feel good, enthusiastic, and happy. Conversely, if one or the other of these things is going badly, they easily fall into depression. None of them has a bigger story within which to set his or her story so as to draw on some meaning beyond the idiosyncratic limits that he or she is experiencing on a given day. Their own story is all they have.

That is a good insight. We don't draw hope from our own stories; we draw it from a much bigger communal story within which our own stories take place. As psychologist James Hollis points out, "Life is never about happiness; it is about meaning. And meaning is only found in the whole picture." He then goes on to quote a cartoon in which a therapist says to the client, "I cannot solve your problem, but I can give you a more compelling story for your misery."

Faith can offer us that more compelling story within which to understand both our miseries and our joys. It sets our lives inside the ultimate meta-narrative, the biggest of all stories. And the need for a meta-narrative becomes especially strong as we age and face more and more marginalization and debilitation. These are crushing realities; it is not easy to make peace, even when we place them within a narrative of faith. But nature itself helps the process because the marginalization and debilitation that come with aging will soon enough let us know that we are no longer in control; we can no longer guarantee our own security, and we must now throw ourselves at the mercy of something bigger than ourselves because now all the wishful thinking and natural optimism in the world are powerless to save us.

From Sophistication to Childlikeness

Central to the message of Jesus is the notion that we must become like little children to enter the kingdom of heaven, but that is easily misunderstood. What does he mean by becoming like a little child? What quality in a child is he idealizing?

When we look at a child, what first touches our hearts is innocence. The innocence of a little child disarms us, judges us, and puts us on guard to be on our best behavior. A baby acts as an exorcist in a room. Innocence is beautiful, but that is not what Jesus is holding up as an ideal to emulate. It is impossible to go through life and remain innocent. Our unstained baptismal robe will not remain spotless unless we die very young. We all are wounded (which is what it means to lose one's innocence), and we all make mistakes.

What Jesus is idealizing in a little child is not innocence but helplessness, the sense that the child cannot provide for herself but needs others. A little child has no illusion of self-sufficiency. Either someone gives her breakfast or there will be no breakfast. We can understand what is at issue here by its opposite. For Jesus, the rich struggle to enter the kingdom of heaven. Why? There is nothing wrong with riches, except that with riches comes the immense, almost irresistible temptation to think that we are self-sufficient, that we have earned what we have, that it hasn't come to us as a gift, and that we are strong enough not to need others. Thomas Aquinas once defined God as "self-sufficient being" and warned us that only God is self-sufficient. Little children have no illusion of self-sufficiency.

What does that mean concretely? Again, the notion is generally fraught with misunderstanding. Childlike does not mean childish. To be childlike does not mean that we protect ourselves from sophistication, that we shield our eyes from seeing things that shatter our belief in Santa, and that we stop our ears from hearing anything that upsets our innocence. Rather, we are meant to learn, to see things as they are (no matter the shattering of our naïveté), to become sophisticated—except that this is only a necessary stage that we pass through and not an end in itself.

I once heard a storyteller put it this way: Imagine you have a two-year-old daughter who asks, "Mommy, where does the sun go at night?" When a child is two years old, don't pull out a globe and try to teach her how the solar system works. Just say, "The sun is tired and it takes a sleep behind the house." But when the child is five or six, that won't work anymore. Now is the time to pull out a globe and some picture books and explain the solar system. That, too, will run its course. When she is in college, it is time to pull out Albert Einstein, Werner Heisenberg, and Max Planck and teach her about relativity and indeterminacy. Then, when she is in graduate school, you need to pull out Stephen Hawking and Brian Swimme and expose her to the unimaginable infinity of space, to the walls of light and black holes in our universe. Then, after all that sophistication, at seventy-five she will know where the sun goes at night: *It is simply tired and takes a sleep behind the house.* What was once childish is now wisdom.

Many thinkers following the renowned French philosopher Paul Ricœur would call this post-sophistication *second naïveté.* An old professor of mine used this example: If you ask a naïve child whether he believes in Santa and the Easter Bunny, he will say yes. If you ask an older child whether he believes in Santa and the

Easter Bunny, he will say no. But if you ask an even brighter child, he will give you a knowing smile and say yes. Sophistication, like the illusion of self-sufficiency, is something we pass through on the road to maturity.

Both conservatives and liberals tend to struggle with the concept of childlikeness, of second naïveté. Conservatives (akin to J. D. Salinger's character Holden Caulfield in *The Catcher in the Rye*) tend to want to shield innocence from being shattered by sophistication. Liberals, for their part, tend to want to make sophistication an end in itself rather than a state one passes through en route to maturity.

One of the challenges of aging is to let the process itself help us move toward second naïveté, post-sophistication, and a childlikeness where, having given up the illusion of self-sufficiency and having studied Albert Einstein and Stephen Hawking, we are ready to believe in Santa and the Easter Bunny again.

From Control to Surrender

Ultimately, all the invitations in the Gospel can be summarized in one word—"surrender." Our final human and spiritual task is to let go and, like Jesus in his final act, hand over our spirits in an act of love and trust. But that is also the most difficult task in life. Everything in us militates against this.

Within all of us, there is a powerful instinctual pressure to take and keep control of our lives, to be masters of our own destinies. That is why it is so difficult to surrender our car keys, to let others take charge of our finances, and to let others make decisions for our lives. Today it is fashionable to chide people for this and call them control freaks, but for most of our lives, this is a very healthy instinct, put there by God and nature. We are meant to be in control of our own lives.

However, while this instinct serves us well for most of our

lives, there will come a time for every one of us when we will have to give up control. Whether on our deathbeds or in some assisted living facility, eventually each of us will have to surrender control, trusting that in this experience of powerlessness we will find new life.

Moreover, this surrender is not to be confused with resignation. Resignation is when we are forced against our will to give something up, and that often results in bitterness. Surrender is when we give something up freely and, like Jesus, say, "No one takes [my life] from me, but I lay it down of my own accord."

Dying is the ultimate surrender in trust, and it besets us uninvited. However, God and nature have arranged that the natural debilitations that come with aging give us lots of practice in letting go, long before our deathbeds. This is a lesson we should not have to learn only by conscription. One of our salient spiritual and human tasks as we age is to learn how to let go, how to surrender, so that the spirit we breathe out with our last breath or (ideally) long before our last breath is one that, like Jesus's last breath, issues forth without bitterness as it says, "Father, into your hands I commend my spirit."

From Achievement to Fruitfulness

There's a real difference between our *achievements* and our *fruitfulness,* between our successes and the actual good that we bring into the world.

What we achieve brings us success, gives us a sense of pride, makes our families and friends proud of us, and gives us a feeling of being worthwhile, singular, and important. We've done something. We've left a mark. We've been recognized. And along with those awards, trophies, academic degrees, certificates of distinction, and artifacts we've left behind come public recognition and respect. Moreover, what we achieve generally produces and leaves behind something that is helpful to others. We can, and should, feel good about our legitimate achievements.

However, achievement is not the same thing as fruitfulness. Our achievements are things we have accomplished. Our fruitfulness is the positive, long-term effect these achievements have on others. Achievement doesn't automatically mean fruitfulness. Achievement helps us stand out; fruitfulness brings blessing into other people's lives.

So, as we enter the last chapters of our lives, we need to ask ourselves these questions: How have my achievements, my successes, the things I'm proud to have done positively nurtured those around me? How have they helped bring joy to other people's lives? How have they helped make the world a better, more loving place? How have any of the trophies I've won or distinctions I've been awarded made those around me more peaceful rather than more restless? This is different from asking how our achievements have made us feel or how they have given us a sense of self-worth or witnessed to our uniqueness.

It's no secret that our achievements, however honest and legitimate, often produce jealousy and restlessness in others rather than inspiration and restfulness. We see this dynamic in how we so often envy and secretly hate highly successful people. Their achievements generally do little to enhance our own lives but instead trigger an edgy restlessness within us. The success of others, in effect, often acts like a mirror in which we see, restlessly and sometimes bitterly, our own lack of achievement. Why?

Generally, there's blame on both sides. On the one hand, instead of stemming from a genuine desire to help others, our achievements are often driven from a self-centered need to set ourselves apart from others, to stand out, to be singular, to be recognized and admired. To the extent that this is true, our successes will trigger envy. On the other hand, our envy of others is often that self-inflicted punishment spoken of in Jesus's parable of the talents, wherein the one who hides his talent gets punished for not using that talent.

The truth is that we can achieve great things without being fruitful, just as we can be very fruitful even while achieving little in terms of worldly success and recognition. Our fruitfulness is often the result not so much of the great things we accomplish but of the graciousness, generosity, and kindness we bring into the world. Unfortunately, our world rarely reckons these as achievements, as accomplishments, as successes. We don't become famous for being gracious. Yet, when we die, while we may well be eulogized for our distinguished achievements, we will be loved and remembered more for the goodness of our hearts. It will be the quality of our hearts, more than our achievements, that will determine how nurturing or asphyxiating the spirits we leave behind are when we're gone. Our real fruitfulness will flow from something beyond the legacy of our accomplishments.

When we distinguish between our achievements and our fruitfulness, we will see that, while death may be the end of our success, productivity, and importance, it isn't necessarily the end of our fruitfulness. Indeed, often our true fruitfulness occurs only after we die, when our spirits can finally flow out more purely. We see that this was true for Jesus. We were able to be fully nurtured by his spirit only after he was gone. Jesus teaches this explicitly in his farewell discourse in John's Gospel when he tells us repeatedly that it's better for us that he goes away because it's only when he's gone that we will be able to truly receive his spirit, his full fruitfulness. The same is true for us. Our full fruitfulness will show only after we have died.

Great achievement doesn't necessarily make for great fruitfulness. Great achievement can give us a good feeling and can make our families and loved ones proud of us. But those feelings of accomplishment and pride are not a lasting or deeply nourishing fruit. Indeed, the good feeling that accomplishment gives us is often a drug, an addiction, that forever demands more and more of us and sets loose envy and restlessness in others as it underscores our separateness. The fruit that feeds love and community tends to come from our shared vulnerability and not from those achievements that set us apart.

As we age, it becomes more important to think about the fruitfulness we can leave behind than the accomplishments we can still achieve in the time left for us.

HOW JESUS SUMMARIZES ALL THIS

All this can be put into shorthand, into one all-encompassing challenge. In the Gospel of Mark, Jesus begins his preaching with words that encapsulate his whole message and serve as an interpretive key to unlock our understanding of that message: "The time is fulfilled, and the kingdom of God has come near; repent, and believe in the good news."

The Greek word for "repent" is *metanoia,* a word that implies infinitely more than what is connoted in its English translation. In common parlance, the word "repent" implies that we have made some mistakes in our lives and now need to have proper contrition and make proper amends for them. For us, to repent is to come back to some lost innocence.

Metanoia connotes something considerably wider. It comes from two Greek words, *meta* (a word we have in English, connoting something higher or something greater than ordinary, such as a meta-narrative) and *nous,* the Greek word for "mind." Hence, *metanoia* means putting on a higher mind, a more noble one, a mind that precisely does not give itself over to pettiness, arrogance, bitterness, wishful thinking, and false sophistication. Also, the word *metanoia* is the antithesis of *paranoia*. Therefore, the opening line of Jesus's preaching might more aptly be rendered, "Put on a higher, more noble mind and begin to trust!"

Some of the early Christian writers affirmed that each of us has two minds, a noble one and a petty one. In each of us there is a noble mind that takes its root in our fundamental identity of being made in God's image and likeness. However, in each of us there is also a wounded, petty, small-hearted, and paranoid mind. At any given moment, we can be hooked to and acting out of one or the other. For instance, one morning getting out of bed, you may feel at your very best in terms of your humanity. At that moment, you feel magnanimous, generous in spirit, empathic with the world, bighearted, noble. You go to work in that state, but at a morning meeting, a co-worker cruelly slights or insults you. Within seconds you feel the doors of your heart slamming shut, and within minutes your magnanimity and nobility of spirit are gone. In an instant you have turned from saintliness to pettiness. Now ask yourself, Which one of those two people is you? They both are! Inside us there are two minds and two hearts. We are both noble and petty, bighearted and bitterly wounded, altruistic and selfish. Jesus's invitation to *metanoia* is an invitation to act out of our higher selves.

Henri Nouwen captures this idea in an utterly simple but profound way in one of his earliest books, *With Open Hands*. He suggests two fundamental postures in our approach to life: *metanoia* and *paranoia*. The symbol of *paranoia* is the image of a clenched fist, one's energy drawn inward, defensive, suspicious, ready to strike out; the symbol of *metanoia* is that of Jesus stretched out on the cross, naked, defenseless, his hands open with nails driven through them. The clenched fist represents all that is wounded, fearful, untrusting, and defensive inside us, whereas the open hand with a nail driven through it represents all that is highest, most noble, trusting, and loving inside us.

In our better moments, we know that, ultimately, our psychological and spiritual task is to bring ourselves to what is highest, most noble, and trusting inside us, and the means to get there are prayer, religious practice, and fidelity in charity in our families and communities. However, too often it does not really happen. For all kinds of reasons, we find ourselves mired in *paranoia,* bitterness, and distrust. Hence, the aging and dying process was designed by God to bring us to *metanoia,* even if we are dragged there screaming.

PART TWO

|||||||||||||||||||||||||||||||||

THE FINAL STAGES OF HUMAN
MATURITY FROM A FAITH PERSPECTIVE

WHEN THE SIGNS OF AGE BEGIN TO MARK MY BODY (AND STILL more when they touch my mind); when the ill that is to diminish me or carry me off strikes from without or is born within me; when the painful moment comes in which I suddenly awaken to the fact that I am ill or growing old; and above all at that last moment when I feel I am losing hold of myself and am absolutely passive within the hands of the great unknown forces that have formed me; in all those dark moments, O God, grant that I may understand that it is You (provided only my faith is strong enough) who are painfully parting the fibres of my being in order to penetrate to the very marrow of my substance and bear me away within Yourself. . . .

Teach me *to treat my death as an act of communion.*

FOUR

|||||||||||||||||||||||||||||||

Passivity as Generativity and Leaving Behind a Nurturing Spirit

A FAITH PERSPECTIVE

What unique perspectives can Christian faith bring to the question of accepting the diminishments that come with aging and allowing them to become a new and deeper modality of generativity in our lives? Can we be generative when we seem helpless to actively give anything to others?

Both Jesus and several renowned Christian mystics offer us some important insights on these questions, insights that (because they are so perplexingly paradoxical) are often hidden from conventional wisdom, even in most circles of faith. What are these paradoxical perspectives?

PASSIVITY AS GENERATIVITY: THE PASSION OF JESUS AS A PARADIGM

We speak of Jesus as both living for us and dying for us, as giving us a double gift: his life and his death. Too often, however, we do not distinguish between the two, lumping them together into one act when, in fact, other than in metaphor, they were two quite distinct things. Namely, Jesus gave his life for us in one way, through his activity; he gave his death for us in another way, through his passivity, his passion.

It is easy to misunderstand what the Gospels present to us as the *passion of Jesus*. The English word "passion," in this case, is a false friend because we spontaneously grasp its meaning in relation to the wrong thing. When we use the word *passion* in relation to Jesus's suffering, we spontaneously connect it to the idea of pain: the pain of the Crucifixion, the scourging, the whips, the nails in his hands, the humiliation before the crowd. And, indeed, the passion of Jesus does refer to this, but that is not the focus here. The English word *passion* takes its root in the Latin *passio*, meaning "passivity," and that is its primary connotation here.

What the passion narratives in the Gospels describe for us is Jesus's passivity—that is, how he gives his death to us through his passivity, through what he absorbed, just as he had given his life to us through his activity, through what he did. Indeed, in three of the Gospels, we can divide the Gospel into two clearly distinct parts. We can split off everything that is narrated *before* Jesus's arrest in the Garden of Gethsemane and call this part *the Activity of Jesus Christ*. Then we can take the section of that Gospel that describes what happens *after* Jesus's arrest and call it *the Passivity of Jesus Christ*. This would help make clear an important distinction—again, that Jesus gave his life for us through his activity but that he gave his death for us through his passivity, and both were very generative.

This is clear in the Gospels. Up until his arrest, the Gospels describe Jesus as active, as doing things: taking charge, preaching, teaching, healing, performing miracles, consoling people. Then, after his arrest, all the verbs become passive. He is led away, manhandled by the authorities, whipped, and helped in carrying his cross. Ultimately, he is nailed to the cross and dies. After his arrest, like a patient in hospice, he no longer does anything; others do it for him and to him. He is passive, a patient.

And this is what needs to be highlighted here: As Christians, we believe that we are saved by Jesus's life, by his *activity,* by what he actively taught us and did for us. But, and this is the paradox, we believe that we are also saved, indeed preeminently so, by his death, by his *passivity,* by what he passively endured. His passivity was in fact more generative than his activity. How can this be understood?

Henri Nouwen, in trying to explain this, shares this story: He once went to a hospital to visit a man dying of cancer. The man was still relatively young, in his sixties, and had been a hardworking and generative person. He was a father and provided well for his family. He was the chief executive officer in a large company and prided himself on taking good care of both the company and his employees. Moreover, he was involved in many other organizations, including his church, and because of his leadership abilities, he was often the one in charge. But now, this once-so-active and generative man, who was used to being in control of things, was lying on a hospital bed, dying, unable to provide for himself, even for some of his most basic needs.

As Nouwen approached the bed, the man took his hand. It is significant to note what particular frustration he expressed and what particular thing he asked for: "Father, you have to help me! I'm dying, and I am trying to make peace with that, but there is something else too. You know me: I have always been in charge. I took care of my family. I took care of the company. I took care of the church. I took care of things! Now I am lying here on this bed with tubes in me, and I can't even take care of myself. Nurses have to bring me a bedpan; I can't even go to the bathroom!

Dying is one thing, but this is another! I'm helpless! I can't do anything anymore!"

Despite his exceptional pastoral skills, Nouwen, like any of us in a similar situation, was left helpless in the face of this man's plea. The man was undergoing his passion, his passivity. He was now a *patient*. (Notice this word also comes from the Latin *passio*.) Just like Jesus, he had once been active, the one in charge; and now, just like Jesus in the hours leading up to his death, he was reduced to being a patient, one who is ministered to by others. Nouwen, for his part, tried to help the man see the connection between what he was undergoing and what Jesus endured in his passion, especially how this time of helplessness, diminishment, passivity, and dying is meant to be a time when we can give to those around us a deeper gift, the gift of our death. Among other things, Nouwen read the passion narratives aloud to him.

In our passivity, we can give to others a gift that we are unable to give in our activity. This is partly mystery, but it is not an entirely abstract idea. Allow me a personal example: I had a sister, Helen, who was an Ursuline nun, and a very happy one. She entered the convent at the age of eighteen and died of cancer more than thirty years later. During most of those thirty years as a religious sister, she worked at a high school for girls run by her order. It was a residential school, and the young women attending it lived in a convent residence during the school year. Helen was in charge of taking care of their needs outside the classroom, and these young women leaned on her for many things. She became a surrogate mother to them, and she loved every minute of it. She had the perfect temperament for the part. She was an extrovert, more of a natural doer than a natural contemplative. She loved activity, loved organizing things, had great common sense, and loved being with people. She also played that role in our family after our parents died. She was the person who took charge. That was her temperament, and she was much loved for it.

Then in her early fifties, she was diagnosed with cancer. After initial surgery and treatment, it seemed as if she had beaten it. She went back to work, to her busy life, to the activities she so loved and in which she thrived. But the cancer eventually returned and claimed her. Moreover, it played a mean trick on her. For the last nine months of her life, this formerly active woman lay in bed, paralyzed from the waist down, unable to prepare her own food, unable to go to the bathroom on her own, unable to do all those generative things she had done for others her entire adult life. For nine months before she died, the exact length of time it takes to gestate new human life, she lay in bed as a patient, in a frustrating passivity, unable to be in charge, even of her own basic needs.

But there is a great irony and stunning biblical parallel in this: During those last months when she was unable to do things for others as she had always done, she, in some deep but real way, was able to give more to those around her than she was able to give during all those years of her busy activity. In that, her life and death in its own humble way paralleled the life and death of Jesus: For most of her life, like Jesus during his active life, she was the active one, busy, generative, doing things for others. In all that activity, she gave her life away. Then, in those months when she lay paralyzed in bed unable to do things for others, she was passive, undergoing her passion. And like Jesus in his passivity, she was generative in a very powerful way.

In a similar vein, a friend of mine shares this story: She grew up one of five children in a home where her father's alcoholism wreaked havoc. By the time her father died, the family was irrevocably fractured and the five children, now adults, were bitterly alienated from one another. Her mother spent the rest of her life attempting to reconcile her children. She tried to gather them for Thanksgiving, Christmas, Easter, and other special occasions, and she worked one-on-one with all of them, cajoling, encouraging, and begging them to reconcile. She spent years of prayer and effort, but she could not effect a reconciliation.

Then she was struck with terminal cancer. In the final week of her life, she was in hospice, and all five of her children gathered round to be with her. She was slipping in and out of consciousness and could speak very little, most times not at all. A surprising thing happened: Her children, sitting mute with her in her helplessness, reconciled with one another. What she was unable to do through years of proactive effort, she was able to do when, seemingly, she could not do anything at all beyond lying helplessly on a hospice bed and passively enduring a disease that was taking her out of this life. Such is the mystery of love and how we give life in what we do for others and in what we endure and absorb.

Our passivity and dying can potentially be our last and greatest gift to others. There is a deep truth in this, which unfortunately we stand in danger of losing. Today, certainly within much of secular culture, we tend to equate value only with utility, action, and work. In a culture that for the most part understands only health and productivity, we find it almost impossible to see value in people who, because of age, health, or handicap, cannot visibly and actively contribute. So we ask ourselves, What is the value of people living with Alzheimer's? What is the value of people continuing to live in palliative care when there is no chance of recovery or improvement and they have already slipped away from us mentally? What is the value of people who are so mentally or physically challenged that by normal standards they cannot contribute anything? The answer lies in the mystery of passivity. Sometimes in our helplessness and passivity, we can give something that is deeper than what we can give through our strength and activity. A culture that is speaking more and more of euthanasia clearly is beginning to lose sight of this and will be significantly impoverished, humanly and spiritually, for that loss.

James Hillman, in his brilliant book *The Force of Character,* highlights the poverty that besets a culture that no longer understands what it receives through the passivity of those whose contribution is of another kind. He asks the question, What is our value to others once our practical usefulness, and perhaps even our sanity, are gone? What do people bring to the table once they can no longer bring what society deems useful? His answer is character, and not just their own. They bring character to others.

Another parallel between what occurred in Jesus's passion and what often occurs in our own diminishment and death is also helpful to highlight. Jesus died by crucifixion. Crucifixion was a death designed by Romans as their version of the death penalty. But, in designing crucifixion, they had more than simple capital punishment in mind. They wanted, at the same time, to inflict the optimal amount of suffering that is possible for a person to endure. Hence, the death was to be slow and torturous. Beyond that, crucifixion was also meant to totally and publicly humiliate the person being executed. Among other things, the person was stripped naked and hung on a cross with his genitals exposed. As well, often at the moment of death, or even before, his bowels would loosen in a further humiliation. Crucifixion was not a pretty sight! Neither is death through old age, cancer, dementia, AIDS, multiple sclerosis, amyotrophic lateral sclerosis (ALS), and countless other diseases. Like death by crucifixion, terminal illnesses also inflict intense pain and, worse still, utterly humiliate the body. They are also not a pretty sight. Terminal illnesses mimic the crucifixion. This should not surprise us, since our diminutions, powerless moments, humiliations, and illnesses are our passion, our crucifixion, the passivity through which we are asked, like Jesus, to give our deaths as our final gift to others.

And how are our deaths received? What is the effect of our passivity on others, if it is given over in a loving manner? Again, Jesus is the paradigm. The Gospel of John tells us that at the moment of Jesus's death, "blood and water" flowed from his dead body. This is a stunning image carrying several levels of meaning. First of all, the image is clearly one of birth: Blood and water accompany the newborn out of the womb. Jesus's death is understood to be giving birth to something in the world. What is being born? The answer is in the symbols, blood and water. What is blood? Blood is the life principle inside us. We are alive when blood flows through us. What is water? Water does two things for us: It quenches our thirst, and it washes us clean. When we combine these concepts, we begin to get a sense of what the Gospel is trying to teach us here. It is telling us what Jesus's disciples experienced in the face of his death. They felt an outpouring of blood and water—that is, a deeper and richer flow of life within themselves and a sense of being both nurtured and cleansed in a new way. They felt something flow out from Jesus's death that made them freer, less guilty, and more open to life than ever before. They felt washed, cleansed, and nourished.

This sounds abstract and quasi-magical, but it is anything but that. We have the same experience when someone we know and love dies in such a way so as to give her death to us. Here are some examples: If someone were to ask me what were the most joy-filled occasions I have been present at in the last ten years, my answer at first glance would seem unreal—a number of funerals, specifically funerals of women and men who in the way they died figuratively set off a flow of blood and water from their caskets.

A couple of years ago, I went to visit a man who was already in palliative care, dying of cancer. He was a young man, still in his fifties, but he was dying well because he was dying in the same way he had lived his life, without bitterness and without enemies. He spoke to me of the intense loneliness of dying: "I have a wonderful wife and kids, and they are holding my hand every minute, but, like Jesus in the Garden of Gethsemane, *I'm a stone's throw away from everyone.* I'm loved, but I'm alone in this. Nobody can be truly with you as you're dying." Then he shared this: "I've had a good life. I have no regrets. I don't have an enemy; at least I don't know of one. And I want to do this right. I want to die with a dignity that makes my wife and kids proud of me. I want to do this right for them and for everyone else."

He died some days later; his family and everyone who knew him were deeply saddened. But in that sadness, there was also something else: an outflow of blood and water. After his funeral, as we walked out of the church to a small reception, there was not one person who knew this man well, including his grieving wife and children, who, at a level deeper than the sadness of the moment, did not feel freer, less guilty, and more open to life than ever before. He wanted to do his death right, and he did, and that reinforced everything good he had done in his life so that what he wanted to give to us came to us: the goodness of his life and the love he showed in his death. Blood and water flowed from his casket to all of us, not least to his family.

Less happily, this is also sometimes true in its opposite: Not every death is a gift to those who knew the person. Many of us have been to funerals where, because of the manner in which the person lived or died, we did not feel blood and water flowing from the casket but rather felt as if the oxygen were being drawn out of the room. Instead of feeling freer, less guilty, and more open to life, we felt guilty about the very act of breathing and guilty about enjoying anything in life. How we live and how we die leave behind a spirit, a blessing or a curse, after we are gone. Our caskets will either emit a flow of life-giving and guilt-freeing blood and water or suck oxygen from the room and from the hearts of those who knew us.

The final human and Christian challenge of our lives is the struggle to give our deaths away.

LEAVING A SPIRIT BEHIND: THE MYSTERY OF GIVING AND RECEIVING SPIRIT

How we live through and absorb our helplessness and passivity, how we give these over, with either love or bitterness, is also deeply entwined with a further mystery: how we give and receive spirit and how we are present and absent to one another.

Presence and absence are not simple notions. We can be deeply present to someone even when we are physically absent and vice versa. There is also the question of the quality of our presence, as blessing or curse, or as binding someone or setting them free. In Christian terms, that is the mystery of Ascension and Pentecost.

For example, when Jesus is saying farewell to his disciples, he tries to explain some of the deep paradoxes in the mystery of presence and absence. He tells them that it is better for them that he goes away because, unless he does, he will be unable to send them his spirit. He assures them, too, that the heaviness and grief they will feel at his leaving is really the pain of giving birth and that this heartache will eventually turn warm and nurturing and will bring them a joy that no one can ever take from them.

That is the language of Ascension and Pentecost, not just as it pertains to Jesus leaving this earth and sending his spirit, but also as it pertains to the mystery of the spirit we give and receive in all our goodbyes, including the goodbye in our own deaths. Among other things, this language points to that perplexing experience we have when we can fully understand and appreciate others only after they go away, just as others can fully understand us and let themselves be fully blessed by us only after we go away. Like Jesus, we can send our spirits only after we go away.

This is not abstract. We experience this everywhere in life: A grown child has to leave home before his parents can fully understand and appreciate him for who he really is. There comes a day in his life when he stands before his parents and, in whatever way he articulates it, says to them, "It is better for you that I go away. Unless I go, you will never really know who I am. You will have some heartache now, but that pain will eventually become warm because I will come back to you in a deeper way." Parents need to say the same thing to their children when they are dying.

We really grasp the essence of another only after she has gone away. When someone leaves us physically, we are given the chance to receive her presence in a deeper way. And the pain and heartache we feel in the farewell are birth pangs, the stretching that comes with giving birth to new life. When someone we love has to leave (to go on a trip, to begin a new life, or to depart from us through death), initially that will feel painful, sometimes excruciatingly so. But when that leaving is necessitated by duty or by life itself, then no matter how hard it is, even if it is death itself that takes away our loved one, eventually she will come back to us in a deeper way, in a presence that is warm, nurturing, and immune to the fragility of normal relationships.

I suspect that many of us have experienced this in the death of someone we loved deeply. For me, this happened at the death of my parents. My mother and father died three months apart when I was twenty-three years old. They were young—too young to die in my view—but death took them anyway, against my will and theirs. Initially, their death was experienced as very painful, as bitter. My siblings and I wanted their presence in the same way we had always had it—physical, tangible, bodily, real. Eventually the pain of their leaving went away and we sensed that our parents—and all that was best in them—were still with us. They were our mom and dad still, except that now their presence was deeper and less fragile than it had been when they were physically with us. They were with us now, real and nurturing, in a way that nobody and nothing could ever take away.

Our presence to one another physically, in touch, sight, and speech, is no doubt the deepest wonder in all of life, and sometimes the only thing we can appreciate as real. But wonderful as that is, it is always limited and fragile. It is limited because it depends upon being physically connected in some way, and it is fragile because separation (physical or emotional) can easily take someone away from us. With everyone we love (parents, spouses, children, friends, acquaintances, colleagues), we are always just one trip, one misunderstanding, one accident, or one heart attack away from losing their physical presence. This was the exact heartache and fear the disciples felt as Jesus was saying goodbye to them, and that is the heartache and fear we all feel in our relationships. We can easily lose one another. But there is a presence that cannot be taken away, that does not suffer from this fragility: the spirit that, because of the inner dictates of love and life, comes back to us whenever we have to be separated from our loved ones. A spirit returns, and it is deep and permanent and leaves a warm, joyous, and real presence that nobody can ever take from us.

Recently I was at a funeral of a woman who was much loved by family, friends, and community, deservedly so. She had a large family and a large heart. She took care of her own and also helped take care of others. She was one of those women who fed the neighborhood and tried to feed the world. Her life and her love had a wide embrace. By any standard she was a great person. Just before her body was taken out of the church, each of her four children gave a short eulogy. Her eldest son gave a brief sketch of the major chronological events in her life; her eldest daughter then shared about her generosity and her propensity to feed every person and dog in the neighborhood; another of her sons shared some of the wonderful rituals she had developed within their family around birthdays and other celebrations; and finally, her youngest daughter gave a eulogy. Her sharing was brief and poignant. She simply stated what we all already knew: This woman, her mother, was an exceptional person. Then, speaking directly to her siblings, nephews, and nieces, she said, "Our mother and our grandmother was a great woman. We don't fully know that yet, but someday we will because she will come to us. She will come to each of us individually, in her own way, respecting who we are and what our lives are, *and we will get her*—get who she really was, get what she gave to all of us in how she lived and in how she died, get how blessed we were to have had her, get that we had this exceptional, wonderful person as our mom and our grandmother. We will get her spirit, and in receiving that, we will drink more deeply from her person."

In receiving Jesus's spirit, his disciples drank more fully from his depth. That is also true for us as his disciples. And it is also true for how we receive the spirits of our loved ones after they die and how others will receive our spirits after our own deaths. If we age well, absorb our passivities well, and die without bitterness and regret, the spirits we leave behind will be nurturing, warm, and cleansing—biblical blood and water.

FIVE

||||||||||||||||||||||||||||||

The Modality and Darkness of Faith in Its Deeper Stages of Maturity

A common soldier dies without fear, yet Jesus died afraid. What are we to make of this?

A LESSON IN FAITH

When the memoirs of Mother Teresa were first published, the world was shocked. They revealed that for the last fifty years of her life, she had struggled painfully to have any sense of God's presence in her life. Her critics felt a certain glee. Underneath it all, they now believed, she was actually an agnostic, doubting the existence of God. Her devotees were confused. How could this happen to her? How could a woman of such exceptional generosity and seeming faith not be secure in her sense of God's existence and providence?

What underlies both these reactions is a failure to understand the deeper dynamics of faith, the distinction between *the reality of our faith* and *the strength of our imagination,* and the ways faith will often manifest itself in its mature stages.

We tend almost always to misunderstand faith. Faith is not dependent on our ability to imagine or not imagine the existence of God on a given day. For example, imagine a day when your sense that God exists is so strong that you have no doubts whatsoever. Conversely, on a different day, you lie in bed, stare into the darkness, have a sickening feeling that God does not exist, and, despite every effort, cannot conjure up any sense that God is real. Does this mean that one day you had a strong faith and another day you had a weak faith? No. It means that one day you had a strong imagination and the other day you had a weak imagination. God's existence is not dependent upon our capacity to imagine it, especially since God is ineffable and, by very definition, beyond all imagination.

When we equate faith with our intellectual capacity to imagine God's existence or affectively feel it, our faith will have many ups and downs. There will be times when we feel we can walk on water and other times when we feel ourselves sinking like a stone; that is because we have a false notion of faith. The reality of faith and our power to imagine God's existence are two very different things, and that can cause confusion and anxiety in our lives.

The renowned spiritual writer Henri Nouwen shares how a painful confusion and anxiety about faith beset him at the death of his mother. Nouwen, who hailed from the Netherlands, was teaching at Yale when he received news that his mother was dying. As he was flying from Boston to Amsterdam to be with his mother in her dying hours, he was naïvely imagining her final moments as a time when she would give a strong witness to faith. He imagined a warm, pious scene, with his mother holding his hand and assuring him of her love, her faith, and her lack of fear of dying. That is not what happened. Inexplicably, at least to Nouwen at that time, she seemed deeply agitated, particularly in regard to her sense of God's reality and presence. Far from being peaceful and offering reassurance, she seemed to be in darkness, insecure, enveloped in doubt, and in need of reassurance.

For Nouwen, this raised the same questions that were raised by Mother Teresa's memoirs. How could this happen? How could someone who had such a deep faith her whole life die in what seemed like despairing doubt? Can a strong faith simply abandon us, on our deathbeds, no less?

Flying back to Boston after his mother's funeral, Nouwen came to realize a different perspective of what had transpired at his mother's death. What she was radiating was not a weak faith but, paradoxically, a particularly robust one. Throughout her life, every day she had been saying this prayer: *Jesus, I want to live like you, and I want to die like you!* Her prayer had been answered. She died as Jesus did, crying out to a God who, at that moment, seemed absent. But how can that make sense? Why would God take away all affective consolation as she was dying? Why, seemingly, did God take it away from Jesus as he was dying?

Why did Jesus cry out as he was dying? Michael J. Buckley, in a passage that has now become famous, gives a certain answer that throws valuable light on how faith works. It can be helpful, he suggests, to compare Socrates and Jesus simply as a comparison in human excellence. Moreover, we can learn something by comparing how they faced their deaths. Socrates went to his death with calmness and poise. He accepted the judgment of the court, contemplated what might face him after death, found no cause for fear, drank the poison, and died. Jesus, much to the contrary, was almost hysterical with fear. He searched for calm and finally, after crying out in what sounds like despair, established control over himself, moved into his death in silence, and died in that lonely isolation, seemingly in the absence of God.

Here, however, is how Buckley assesses this:

> I once thought that the difference was because Socrates and Jesus suffered different deaths, the one so much more terrible than the other, the pain and agony of the cross so overshadowing the release of the hemlock. But now I think that this explanation, though correct as far as it goes, is superficial and secondary.
>
> I believe now that Jesus was a more profoundly weak man than Socrates, that is, more liable to suffering, to physical pain, and to disheartening weariness; more sensitive to human rejection and contempt; more affected by love and hate. Socrates never wept over Athens. Socrates never expressed sorrow and pain over the betrayal of friends. He was self-possessed and integral, never overextended, convinced that the just man could never suffer genuine hurt. And for this reason, Socrates—one of the greatest, most heroic persons ever to exist, a paradigm of what humanity can achieve within the individual—was a philosopher. And for the same reason, Jesus of Nazareth was a priest—ambiguous, suffering, mysterious, and salvific.

In the view of Kathleen Dowling Singh, if we look at Jesus's last hours through the lens of Kübler-Ross's five stages of grief, we see that after his struggle in the Garden of Gethsemane, he reaches the stage of *Acceptance*. But we can observe two more stages after that. Shortly before he dies on the cross, he cries out in what, from the outside, sounds like despair: "My God, my God, why have you forsaken me?" Then, in a further movement, *he bows his head and gives up his spirit.* His final surrender is clearly something deeper still than his acceptance, and it comes only after he has cried out to a God who seems to have abandoned him.

This is not easy to understand, and we should not be naïve about how the dynamics of faith work and why sometimes, perhaps particularly when we are being most faithful, we experience the *silence of God* or what the mystics call a *dark night of faith.* When we look at the experiences of Mother Teresa through this lens, the question is no longer how this could happen to a person of such deep faith. Rather, the better question is how this could *not* happen. Why would she not experience this darkness? She was an extraordinary woman, a spiritual athlete, someone who had given her entire freedom over to God; might we not then expect this to happen to her? If this is what happened to Jesus, why would it not happen to her? The same might be asked about Henri Nouwen's mother and anyone of deep faith.

What exactly is this experience? What is a *dark night of faith*?

THE DARK NIGHT OF FAITH

A dark night of faith is an experience in which all our felt sense of God dries up and disappears. All our former securities of how we imagined God's existence, understood faith, understood ourselves, and prayed dry up, and we are left in a painful state of unknowing and insecurity about the things of faith and the things of God. At the level of feeling and imagination, none of our former images of faith will give us sustenance anymore. It will feel as if some switch has been shut off and God does not exist. We will feel agnostic, even atheistic. In our minds, we will no longer be able to imagine that God exists; in our hearts, we will no longer be able to conjure up any warm feelings about God or faith; and in our guts, we will lose all sense of security and control in terms of God and faith. We will feel unmoored, distant from the reality of a God we once could imagine and a faith we once had warm feelings about and felt secure in. And from Jesus and the mystics, we learn that a number of other feelings will also accompany all this.

First, this will be excruciatingly painful, like no other pain we have ever experienced. Second, we will feel that there is something wrong with us, that this is happening to us because of some infidelity on our part. Thomas Keating, the renowned spiritual writer on contemplative prayer, shares how on a number of occasions, a person struggling with a dark night of faith would come to him for counsel and invariably ask this question: "What's wrong with me?" He would answer, "God is wrong with you!" Third, we will feel a painful sense of aloneness in our struggle, and the consolation of friends and spiritual directors will not assuage a pain and confusion that feels like despair. Like Jesus in the Garden of Gethsemane, we will feel ourselves "a stone's throw" from everyone, *unanimity minus one.*

We do not get to choose when or where this hits us. Moreover, if Jesus and the mystics are to be believed, it will seek out and hit our Achilles' heel, afflicting us at the one place that is particularly humbling for us. Dark nights of faith are not glamorous; they are humiliating. Jesus was hanging naked and writhing on a cross when he cried out in seeming despair. There is no greater humiliation than this.

Then, as all this is happening, we will have the constant temptation to try to go back to where we once were in our faith and find again the security we once experienced. But, the mystics assure us, this will not work. Why? Because it has already worked! The feelings, the prayer, the sense of God, and the sense of faith we once had have already done their work. They have brought us to the place where it is time to move from image to reality, from possessiveness to love, from security and control to hope.

What is happening inside all our doubt, pain, and confusion? At this stage in our faith development, *what seems like darkness is not, in fact, the absence of light; it is excessive light.* Excessive light, too, causes blindness. We cannot see when there isn't any light, but we also cannot see when we are looking straight into the sun. In a dark night of faith, God is not withdrawing or disappearing; God is breaking through to us so that our imaginative constructs (the PowerPoint pictures of God through which we have nurtured ourselves) now seem unreal and empty because the reality that is breaking through is showing them to be precisely unreal and empty. Our imaginative, flawed images of an infinite and ineffable God are being exorcised by an actual in-breaking of that ineffable God, though at a level of imagination and feeling that is such an overpowering light that it feels like a black darkness. But God is actually flowing into our lives more strongly than ever before. How is this possible, since at the level of feeling, the opposite seems to be happening?

Recall the image in chapter 3, where young fish at the bottom of the ocean ask their mother, "Where is this water everyone talks about? Show us water," and a tech-savvy mother fish responds by setting up a PowerPoint and showing them slides of water. Initially, once the projector is turned off, having conceptualized water only through those PowerPoint pictures, these young fish would struggle to relate to water beyond the now-gone pictures and would feel very insecure about believing that they are swimming in water. For them, this would be a dark night of faith, not because the reality has withdrawn or ceased to exist, but, ironically, because it is now present in such a total way. For as Scripture tells us, in God "we live and move and have our being."

WHAT IS BEING TRANSFORMED?

This is a liminal space; nothing affords us a better opportunity to move to deeper maturity in our faith. The experience is paradoxical; we feel as if we are falling apart even as at a deeper level we are firming up. This is what distinguishes a dark night experience from an emotional or moral depression. An emotional or moral depression drains us of energy (and generally drains a room of energy as well), whereas a religious dark night brings a rich, new (though different) energy into one's life and into a room. That is why, for instance, no one around Mother Teresa had any inkling about what she was undergoing. She brought energy into a room. That is what a dark night does. An emotional or moral depression does the opposite because it turns a person inward, marinating in an unhealthy self-focus, whereas a dark night of faith turns a person outward and helps break her narcissism.

Since in this situation we die to images, a dark night of faith mimics the experience of dying. Notice, however, that this dying takes place at the level of the imagination and of feelings. God doesn't disappear or cease to exist. What disappears are our former feelings about God and our former capacity to imagine God's existence.

God exists, independent of our feelings. Sometimes our heads and hearts are in tune with that and we feel its reality with fervor. Other times our heads and hearts cannot attune themselves to think, imagine, and feel the existence and love of God, and so what we feel inside is precisely a certain absence, a void. But this is a liminal space. The projector has been turned off, the Power-Point images of God are gone, and we are given the opportunity to swim in the reality, as opposed to naïvely thinking the Power-Point slides in our heads and hearts are real.

SOME BIBLICAL IMAGES: METAPHORS ILLUMINATING THE INNER DYNAMICS OF FAITH WHEN IT IS UNDERGOING RADICAL PURIFICATION

While popular spirituality has often been weak in articulating all this, our Scriptures are replete with images of dark nights of faith. The examples are too many to list, but I will highlight a few.

ABRAHAM AND SARAH

When Abraham was eighty years old and Sarah was seventy and post-menopausal, God asked them, against all common sense, to set out for an unknown destination, promising that they would have a child when they got there. Then, after twenty years, when Sarah was ninety and beyond all biological possibility of becoming pregnant, she became pregnant and they had a child. Those twenty years of journey, of trust in a promise that made no sense at all to the human mind and imagination, was a dark night of faith for them, a time when they simply had to swim in the water with nothing within known human experience to lean on.

THE ISRAELITES WANDERING FOR FORTY YEARS IN THE DESERT

This is another biblical image regarding how our faith needs to be purified by undergoing dark nights. In the Book of Exodus, we read the story of Israel leaving Egypt to travel toward the promised land. The story begins with them at a high point in their faith. Having just experienced a miracle that freed them from slavery, the Israelites now expected that God's presence would always be this tangible. It was not to be. Against every expectation they had, God's presence now took on a very different form; at the level of feeling and imagination, God seemed to have abandoned them, died, withdrawn. It took them forty years (biblical code for the length of time required to get the lesson) to understand that God was present to them now in a different modality, a deeper one, in which they had to learn that seeming absence can actually mean deep presence.

After they finally got the lesson, they understood that feeling lost and insecure is a deep, mature place of faith.

The Babylonian Captivity

After a time, the Israelites' faith needed another purification. When Israel entered the promised land, God promised to be with them and promised them three signs of his presence and fidelity: He would give them a *land,* a *king,* and a *temple.* It took some generations, but eventually the Israelites had all three. And these became the anchors for their faith. God was real because God had promised these three things, and they now had them all.

It was not to last! In 598 BCE, the Assyrians came and conquered the land, killed the king, knocked down the temple to its last stone, and deported the entire population to Babylon. So now the Israelites found themselves without a land, a king, or a temple—and seemingly without God. They began to lament: Where is God when everything that guarantees God's presence is gone? God's answer to them: *You will find me again when you search for me at a deeper place, a place beyond your limited expectations, imagination, and feelings.*

An idol is an icon that we have hung on to for too long. Maturing in faith is a lifelong journey of letting go of "a land, a king, and a temple" (icons upon which we can temporarily anchor our faith) to find God at a deeper place, a place beyond icons, a place closer to bedrock, a place closer to full divine presence.

Jesus's Disciples on the Road to Emmaus

This is an image from the Gospels that describes how the faith of Jesus's first disciples needed to be purified. The setting is two days after Jesus's death; two of his disciples are walking away from Jerusalem in depression toward Emmaus, a village seven miles distant. They meet Jesus on the road but fail to recognize him. He asks them why they are despondent, and they share how disillusioned they are because, against every expectation they'd had of Jesus, he was humiliated and crucified by the Romans. Jesus patiently tries to deconstruct and then reconstruct their imagination to make room inside their understanding for a messiah, a God, who can be present, all-powerful, and all-loving in ways beyond their limited expectations of what constitutes success or failure and what constitutes God's presence or absence. Indeed, it is for this reason—their false concept of what constitutes success or failure and God's presence or absence—that they could not recognize Jesus as he was walking beside them. It wasn't that his physical appearance was now so different from his pre-resurrection physical appearance. Rather, they could recognize God only in one set of imaginative constructs.

If we identify God's presence only with warm feelings, fulfilled expectations, and a secure sense that God is present, we will sometimes, like the two disciples walking toward Emmaus, be walking away from our faith dream, feeling desolate that the God we believed in has been crucified and being unable to recognize the God who is walking beside us.

Our journey into maturity in faith is often a walk from Jerusalem to Emmaus. The God of our expectations has been crucified, but God is walking beside us, trying to talk us out of our depression.

JESUS ON THE CROSS IN THE GOSPEL OF MARK

This is a powerful text, easily given over to false interpretation, either through misguided piety or through misunderstanding. This is the image: As he hangs dying on the cross, Jesus cries out, "My God, my God, why have you forsaken me?" The false interpretation from misguided piety is that Jesus really didn't mean those words, that he was not feeling his Father's absence but was only mouthing them for our benefit. That interpretation honors neither the text nor Jesus. The other misunderstanding, coming from agnostic iconoclasts, tells us that Jesus, in the end, died an atheist, no longer believing in God. So, what do his words mean? What was Jesus experiencing on the cross as he cried out in this way? He was experiencing the ultimate dark night of faith. He was feeling the reality of God, but of a God who cannot be imagined, affectively possessed, or held within human security—that is, a God who is ineffable and can ultimately be reached only in faith, charity, and hope.

God wasn't absent to Jesus as he hung on the cross. On the contrary, God was present in such a way that his presence couldn't be manipulated, distorted, or mixed with any idols—imaginative constructs, self-serving affectivity, or false securities. In this kind of darkness, one can no longer project and create a God who is in one's own image and likeness. In this experience, God's presence is pure and unadulterated and is *known* rather than affectively felt and imaginatively grasped. In simple terms, it is so real that it seems unreal. God is so overwhelmingly present that God seems

absent, akin to looking straight into the sun and seeing overpowering light as darkness.

God doesn't handle people on a conveyor belt, so one size
doesn't necessarily fit all. Hence, not everyone will experience
this kind of radical dark night of faith. But we need to be careful what we pray for. If, like Nouwen's mother and Mother Teresa, we pray to be like Jesus and to be one with him in our
living and our dying, we might (in a very mature moment in
our faith journey) find ourselves crying out, *My God, my God,
why have you forsaken me?*

PAUL'S DESOLATION IN 2 CORINTHIANS

At a time in his life when a lot of things were falling apart, the
Jesuit scientist and spiritual writer Pierre Teilhard de Chardin
wrote a letter to his religious superior explaining himself and
his feelings. He was an aging man, exiled from his own country,
silenced by his own church, forbidden to publish his religious
writings, and generally misunderstood by both his ecclesial
community and the world at large. It was a dark time in his life.
However, as he shares in this letter, even as his outer world was
falling apart, inside something else was happening. He tells his
religious superior that, despite all this outer chaos, he is finding
himself "[riveted] ever more firmly to three convictions which
are the very marrow of Christianity."

His words are reminiscent of words that Saint Paul wrote at
a time in his ministry when his outer world also was falling apart.
At a certain time in his life, much like Teilhard de Chardin, he
was experiencing a lot of misunderstanding. A community of
faith he had poured out his soul to build was threatening to turn
against him and disintegrate. He is understandably discouraged.
However, he describes the experience as paradoxical. Even as his

outer world is falling apart, he feels his inner world firming up. This is what a purification of faith feels like.

WHAT SHOULD WE DO WHILE IN A DARK NIGHT OF FAITH?

What can we glean from the deep wells of Christian spirituality when we are undergoing a dark, painful maturation in our faith? The wisdom of Scripture, the saints, and the mystics suggests ten counsels:

1. *Trust.* Trust God's word, trust the witness of Jesus and the saints, trust your own deeper call, and trust that what is happening to you is purifying your faith of projection and your person of selfishness.

2. *Accept what is happening and stay with the pain.* Recognize the wisdom given in the Book of Lamentations: Sometimes all you can do is "put [your] mouth to the dust" and wait.

3. *Accept the unknowing.* The renowned mystic and doctor of the soul John of the Cross tells us that the movement into deeper spiritual and psychological maturity is predicated on learning to understand more by not understanding than by understanding.

4. *Avoid tonics that offer some temporary escape.* This is a passage of growth that must be undergone. Finding means to avoid facing it only delays the inevitable and keeps us at a certain level of immaturity and self-centeredness.

5. *Avoid the "friends of Job."* When Job was undergoing his faith crisis, his well-meaning friends kept telling him

that he must be doing something wrong. *They* couldn't have been more wrong. As Thomas Keating told people undergoing this kind of darkness, "There's nothing wrong with you. God is wrong with you."

6. *Don't be intimidated by spiritual novices.* Spiritual novices, like Job's friends, will tell you that something is wrong, since they believe you should be on a spiritual high all the time. Their counsel is akin to a young couple on their honeymoon giving advice to a mature married couple. A honeymoon is not a mature marriage. Intense fervor is not a mature faith.

7. *Grieve.* Grieve the fervor you once had. Accept the sadness of your own inadequacy, your wounds, your pain, your loss of control, your insecurity. Sadness is not the opposite of meaning and happiness.

8. *Pray.* Keep praying no matter how dry, boring, and routine your prayer is. Pray prayers of familiarity. This is also a time to become bold in prayer, to wrestle with God.

9. *Seek out sound spiritual companions.* This is a time when spiritual direction from an experienced spiritual director (namely, someone who has already undergone this) can be not only helpful but also necessary.

10. *Remain faithful.* Keep showing up! Keep showing up for prayer, for church, for your family, for your friends, for your work, for everything in life, knowing that you are not simply going through the motions but that deep changes are happening under the surface.

WHAT DARK NIGHTS OF FAITH EFFECT WITHIN US

Our aging and growth in life have certain discernible stages. So, too, does our maturing in faith. In our relationship with God, just like in our relationships with one another, we go through three stages: *fervor, boredom, darkness*. Each of these has its own importance and meaning, and each is part of normal growth toward deeper maturity.

I suspect we already know what fervor, the delightful early stage in relationships, does for us. And it should not be trivialized or denigrated in the name of deeper maturity. God gives us fervor for a holy purpose. Most miracles begin with falling in love. Nothing on this earth is as powerful emotionally as falling in love, and this has a singular power to change a heart. Fervor is a good thing, though a first thing.

Two further stages, boredom and darkness, are not as naturally understood. What miracles do they effect within us? In brief, boredom moves us from the surface to the depth, and darkness purifies us from forever creating God and others in our own image and likeness. Let's look at each of these in turn.

Boredom and Tedium: Moving Us from the Surface to the Depth

Imagine this: You are the dutiful daughter or son, and your mother is widowed and in an assisted living facility. You happen to be living close by, while your sister is living across the country, thousands of miles away. So the weight falls on you to be the one to take care of your mother. You dutifully visit her each day. Every afternoon on your way home from work, you stop and spend an hour with her while she has her early dinner. And you do this faithfully, five times a week, year after year.

As you spend this hour each day with your mother, year after year, how many times each year will you have a truly stimulating and deep conversation? Once? Twice? Never? What are you talking about each day? Trivial things: the weather, your favorite sports team, what your kids are doing, the latest show on television, her aches and pains, and the mundane details of your own life. Occasionally you might even doze off for a while as she eats her dinner. In a good year, perhaps once or twice the two of you will share more deeply about something of importance; but save for that rare occasion, you will simply be filling the time each day with superficial conversation.

But—and this is the question—are those daily visits with your mother superficial, mere duty, because your conversations aren't deep? Are you simply going through the motions of an intimate relationship because of duty? Is anything deep happening?

Compare this with your sister who is conveniently living across the country and comes home once a year to visit your mother. When she visits, both she and your mother are wonderfully animated; they embrace enthusiastically, shed tears upon seeing each other, and seemingly talk about things beyond the weather, their favorite sports teams, and their own tiredness. It seems that in this once-a-year meeting they have something that you, who visit daily, do not have. But is this true? Is what's happening between your sister and your mother in fact deeper than what is occurring each day when you visit your mother?

Absolutely not. What they have is, no doubt, more emotional, but it is, at the end of the day, not particularly deep. When your mother dies, you will know your mother better than anyone else knows her, and you will be much closer to her than your sister was. Why? Because through all those days when you visited her and seemed to talk about nothing beyond the weather, deeper things were happening under the surface. When your sister visited your mother, things were happening on the surface (though emotionally the surface can look wonderfully more intriguing than what lies beneath it—that is why honeymoons look better than marriage).

What your sister had with your mother is what novices experience in prayer and what couples experience on a honeymoon. What you had with your mother is what people experience in prayer and relationships when they are faithful over a long period of time. At a certain level of intimacy in all our relationships, including our relationship with God in prayer, the emotions (wonderful as they are) will become less and less important and simple presence—just being together—will become paramount. Previously, the relationship was developing on the surface, and emotions were important; now deep bonding is happening beneath the surface, and emotions recede in importance.

Too often, both popular psychology and popular spirituality do not really grasp this and consequently confuse the novice for the proficient, the honeymoon for the marriage, and the surface for depth. In all our relationships, we cannot make promises as to how we will always feel, but we can make promises to always be faithful, to show up, to be there, even if we are only talking about the weather, our favorite sports team, the latest television program, or our own tiredness. And it is okay occasionally to fall asleep because, as Thérèse of Lisieux once said, a little child is equally pleasing to its parents whether awake or asleep—probably more so asleep! That also holds true for prayer. God does not mind us occasionally napping while in prayer because we are there and that is enough. The great Spanish doctor of the soul John of the Cross tells us that as we travel deeper into any relationship, be it with God in prayer, with each other in intimacy, or with the community at large in service, eventually the surface will be less emotive and *the deeper things will begin to happen under the surface.*

FAITH'S DARKNESS AS PURIFYING US FROM FOREVER CREATING GOD AND OTHERS IN OUR OWN IMAGE AND LIKENESS

A cynic once said that God made us in his own image and likeness and we have never ceased to return the favor. There is more truth to that statement than most of us believers would like to admit. Indeed, that wisecrack is simply street language for the powerful critiques of religion and faith that have been made through the centuries, most notably by critics like Nietzsche, Feuerbach, Marx, and Freud.

Their critique of Christianity, religion, and faith argues along these lines: What we call faith, prayer, and religious worship is simply human projection. We create a God in our image and likeness and then conveniently use him to serve our own aims and needs. There is no God, save for the one we have created. The God we believe in and believe we are praying to is simply a projection of ourselves and our needs.

How true is that? Certainly, when one looks at the history of religion, an argument can be made that this criticism is true. From the first people who made a totem pole and worshipped it to what we see everywhere in our world today, there is depressing evidence that our faith, our churches, and our religions serve us more than they serve God, truth, and love. Nearly everywhere, religion is being used for personal gain, ideological and political purposes, and the undergirding of racism, bigotry, intolerance, and most everything else that is the antithesis of God, truth, and love. It is hard to argue against the fact that a lot of projection masks itself as faith, church, and religion.

But—and this is the point—there is also overwhelming evidence to the contrary. Faith, church, and religion have also produced, and are still producing, powerful witnesses to a transcendent God who cannot be manipulated for our own purposes, witnesses to a truth beyond self-interest, and witnesses to a love that is selfless. That, too, cannot be argued against. So, where does that leave us?

Looking at these two sets of evidence, the renowned spiritual author Michael J. Buckley makes this comment: In their critique of faith and our religious practices, Nietzsche, Feuerbach, Marx, and Freud are 90 percent correct. Moreover, they are doing us a favor by pointing out that much of our religious practice is actually projection. Religion needs critics of this kind in order to see its own blind spots. However, while these critics are 90 percent right, *they are 10 percent wrong, and that makes all the difference.* In that 10 percent where pure religious experience occurs, God has been able to flow into our Scriptures, our faith, our lives, our self-understanding, our churches, and our worship. While a lot of religious experience and religious practice is far from pure, some is—and that makes all the difference.

What accounts for the 10 percent? When are those rare times when we are not projecting and creating God in our image and likeness but are letting God flow into our lives without contamination from self-interest? That 10 percent occurs precisely at those times when we are experiencing in all its radicality a dark night of faith, when all our faculties—head, heart, and gut—lie silenced, helpless, unable to imagine, feel, or safeguard our security. When that happens, God can flow into our lives and into this world purely, uncontaminated by human projection and self-interest, because in our frustrating darkness we are helpless to control the experience.

Why does God give us dark nights of faith? Why did Jesus suffer this while hanging on the cross? Why did Mother Teresa and Henri Nouwen's mother undergo such painful darkness when they had been so habitually faithful? So that this 10 percent could happen, so that God could flow purely into a human life without being contaminated by human projection

PART THREE

||||||||||||||||||||||||||||||||

LOOKING FOR A BEGGAR'S HUT, LEAVING THE FOREST, AND GIVING OUR DEATHS AWAY

THE DEVELOPMENTAL TASKS OF LATE LIFE: THE FURTHER CULTIVA-tion of emotional, cognitive, and spiritual gifts, the softening and opening of the heart, the call to service, and the cultivation of pure awareness.

SIX

Forest Dwelling and Preparing to Find Our Beggar's Hut

God is being built. I too have applied my tiny red pebble, a drop of blood, to give Him solidity lest He perish—so that He might give me solidity lest I perish. I have done my duty.

SEARCHING FOR A VOCABULARY

We have a word that names and defines the stage in life between childhood and adulthood. We call it adolescence. But we have no such word to name and define the stage between initial retirement and that final stage in life (perhaps as much as twenty-five or thirty years later) when, because of failing health, failing energy and circumstance, we face marginalization, isolation, assisted living, dementia, palliative care, hospice, and death. We are developing a vocabulary for that stage in life, but it is still a work in progress.

As we saw earlier, Hindu anthropology and spirituality do

have a term for this. They call it Forest Dwelling and understand
it as a period of stepping away from our former duties, and perhaps even our homes, to spend time trying to create a vision of
how to be generative in a way in which we now give something
different to the world and prepare ourselves for that time when
things like marginalization, isolation, assisted living, dementia,
and hospice will, whether we like it or not, turn us into holy beggars who, now helpless as young children, live without any illusion of self-sufficiency.

What is being asked of us psychologically during this time?
What is being asked of us spiritually? Nature and God always
have an intention written into our DNA, body and soul, for every
season of our lives. What is the intention for this season of life,
one that we are still struggling to recognize, name, and define? In
Hindu terms, this is a time to sort out how to move from the
home and security we have built for ourselves to a "beggar's hut,"
a place beyond self-sufficiency. We all will eventually have to
move there, either voluntarily or because it has been imposed on
us by circumstance or failing health. Anthropologically, this is the
time when we are invited to become fully mature Elders. In
Christian terms, this is a time to bring God's compassion and
smile to the world.

THE INVITATION INNATE IN THIS STAGE OF LIFE:
TO BECOME MATURE ELDERS

What are we to learn in the mythic forest? What invitations are
innate in this season of our lives? There are many, but ultimately
they are one. We are invited to become mature Elders, Sophias.
Becoming mature Elders asks us to become women and men who
turn aging into a natural monastery, carry tension for the young, offer
prophecy to the world, radiate God's compassion, work at rescuing

God from narrowness, bless the young and bring God's smile to the world, give up on fear, and proactively prepare to move to a place beyond the illusion of self-sufficiency: the beggar's hut. Let's look at each of these in turn.

Turning Aging into a Natural Monastery

What is a monastery? How do monasteries work? Saint Benedict (AD 480–547), who is considered the founder of Western monasticism, offered this counsel as an essential rule for his monks: "Stay in your cell and it will teach you everything." Properly understood, this is a rich metaphor, not a literal counsel. When he says this, he is not referring to a literal cell in a monastery. He is referring to the state of life in which a monk or anyone else finds himself.

Sometimes this has been expressed in Christian spirituality as being faithful to *one's duties of state.* The idea here is that if a person is faithful to the situation in life in which she finds herself, life itself will bring her to maturity and virtue. For example, a mother who gives herself over in selflessness and fidelity to raising her children will be brought to maturity and altruism through that process. Her home will be her monk's cell, and she will metaphorically be the abbess of the monastery (with some very young monks). Staying inside that monastery, her home, will teach her all she needs to know. She will be raising children, but they will also be raising her. Motherhood will turn her into a wise Elder, a biblical and archetypal Sophia.

The process of aging is a natural monastery. If we live long enough, eventually the aging process turns us all into monks. Monks take four vows: poverty, chastity, obedience, and perseverance. The process of aging, which moves us (seemingly without mercy) toward marginalization and dependence on others, away from an active sex life, and into a living situation such as a nursing home, imposes those four vows on us. But, as Saint Benedict counsels, this can teach us all we need to know, and it has a unique power to mature us in a very deep way. Monks have secrets worth knowing. So does the aging process.

This can be particularly instructive for how we can make our final days and our deaths a more radical gift to others. In the first centuries of Christianity, martyrdom was considered the ideal way for a Christian to end his days on earth. It was seen as a radical way of imitating Christ and giving one's death away as a gift. Of course, this had to be rethought after Christianity became the state religion and emperors no longer martyred Christians. What followed were various attempts at metaphorical martyrdom. One fairly popular method was that after raising their children and reaching retirement, a couple would leave each other and go off to separate monasteries to live out the rest of their lives as a monk and a nun.

Classical Christian mystics speak about how in the last phase of our lives we should enter something they call the *dark night of the spirit*—namely, that we proactively make a radical decision grounded in faith to move into a situation in life where we can no longer take care of ourselves but must trust, in raw faith, that God will provide for us. This parallels Hindu spirituality, which suggests that in the last, fully mature stage of life we should become *sannyasins,* holy beggars.

I suspect that most of us will never proactively cut off all our former securities and, on purpose, place ourselves in a situation in which we are helpless to provide for and take care of ourselves. But this is where nature steps in. The aging process will do it for us. It will turn us into *sannyasins* and put us in the *dark night of the spirit.* As our health declines and we find ourselves more marginalized in terms of having a vital place within society, we will progressively lose our capacity to take care of ourselves. Eventually, if we live long enough, most of us will move into an assisted living facility, which is, in effect, a natural monastery.

What an apt metaphor! The metaphor is also apropos for what it means to (by conscription) enter the *dark night of the spirit* and to be a holy beggar, a *sannyasin.* In essence, it means this: When someone is in an assisted living facility, regardless of whether she is a millionaire or a pauper, the rules are the same for everyone. Since she can no longer take care of herself (and indeed doesn't have to), she lives a monastic life of obedience and dependence. In assisted living, she lives by the monastic bell and dies as a holy beggar.

Carrying Tension for the Young

One of the primary tasks of an Elder is to help carry the young— that is, help them carry their struggles, their triumphs, their mortgages, and their tensions. How can we carry tension for the young or for anyone?

The Gospels have a concept for this. They call it *pondering.* The word is initially used to describe what Mary, the mother of Jesus, was forced to do at moments in her life. She was forced to ponder certain things in her heart, as when she was told that she would become pregnant by the Holy Spirit and when she was told by Simon that a sword would pierce her heart. What is meant by that? Some English versions translate this from its original Greek with the word *treasured,* implying that Mary was careful to truly remember what happened at that moment. That, no doubt, is part of its meaning. But there is more.

To understand what it means to ponder in the biblical sense, we need to make a key distinction: One can ponder in the Greek sense, and one can ponder in the Hebrew sense. Pondering in the Greek sense might aptly be defined by an expression that comes to us from Greek philosophy: *The unexamined life is not worth liv-*

ing. Our commonsense way of thinking is very much tied to that notion of pondering, where to ponder means to try to think something through in all its depth and implications. One pictures, for example, Rodin's famous sculpture of the thinker, someone sitting in a chapel or on a mountainside, intensely reflecting on something, mulling it over, considering all its various angles. This is what the word would mean had the Gospels been written by Aristotle. But the Gospels, while written in Greek, express Hebrew thought, in which pondering has a different, more existential connotation. Simply put, to ponder in the Hebrew sense means *to hold, carry, and transform tension so as not to give back in kind, knowing that whatever energies we do not transform, we will transmit.*

This can be understood by looking at its opposite. In the Gospels, the opposite of pondering is not to "not ponder" but to "be amazed." Notice in the Gospels how often a crowd who is reacting to something Jesus said or did is described with the words "and they were amazed." (This occurs frequently in Luke's Gospel in reaction to the miracles of Jesus.) Jesus is rarely happy with this reaction. It is in essence a mindless reaction; a crowd simply lets an energy flow through it. Crowds tend to do that, and so do we.

With an apology that these images are more mechanical than soulful, allow me to contrast the biblical image of pondering with the biblical image of amazement. An image for amazement is that of an electrical wire. It simply lets the energy flow through it: 120 volts in, 120 volts out. An image for pondering is that of a water purifier. A water purifier does not simply let things flow through it. It takes in contaminated water—water filled with toxins, dirt, impurities, and poisons—holds those contaminants inside itself, and gives out pure water. That's the biblical image of pondering, and the invitation to do that is the penultimate invitation for coming to human maturity.

The process of aging is a crucible that holds us inside a purifying fire. The intent of that fire is to bring us to a level of maturity where we are more focused on helping others deal with the tension in their lives than we are concerned with the tension in our own lives. That is the mark of a true Elder.

How do we help others carry tension? How do we take tension out of a community? By absorbing the tension in the same way a water purifier removes toxins from water. By taking in conflict, misunderstanding, bitterness, polarization, immaturity, and sin; holding those poisons and toxins inside ourselves; and giving back only empathy, graciousness, maturity, and virtue. How badly this is needed! How vital the role of a true Elder!

We are part of countries, communities, churches, families, and friendships that are full of tension. Misunderstanding, bitterness, accusation, and anger are everywhere. The task of an Elder is to say, "The gossip stops with me; the bitterness stops with me; the anger stops with me; the accusations stop with me. I will absorb those energies instead of retransmitting them. I will be a scapegoat who helps take away the tension inside a community by absorbing it."

OFFERING PROPHECY TO THE WORLD

Who and what is a prophet? Three things are essential in defining what makes a prophet. First, a prophet doesn't foretell the future; a prophet properly names the present as God is seeing it. And since God is on the side of the poor, a prophet names present reality from the viewpoint of the poor. Second, a prophet makes not a vow of alienation but a vow of love. A prophet is recognized by his deep empathy. Third, a prophet is never partisan but is also never private. A prophet recognizes that the private deeply affects the public.

And who are the poor for whom the prophet speaks? Is it the economically poor? The politically oppressed? Refugees on borders? Victims of violence? Those suffering humiliation? The emotionally distraught? Those contemplating suicide? Those forced to do hard labor? Children? The dying? The elderly who are marginalized and moving toward death?

Who is poor? Jesus has, I believe, an answer that takes in all these categories. For him, the poor are those who, for whatever reason, virtue, or circumstance, have no illusion of self-sufficiency. That is why he tells us the little children are privy to the secret of the kingdom. In singling out little children as paradigms of what we are meant to be, he is not (as is the popular conception) idealizing their innocence, morally stunning though that is. What he is holding up as an ideal is their contingency—that is, the fact that they do not have any illusion of self-sufficiency. They are dependent on others and on things beyond themselves. They are not self-sufficient. They are the biblically poor.

The marginalization that eventually comes with aging is a privileged way to move into solidarity with the poor, to recognize more deeply something we should have recognized our whole lives: We are not self-sufficient; we need others. From that recognition, from accepting our place among the poor, we can now be prophetic. And what is to be our message? What are we, in love, to name?

We are to name what Jesus names in the first words of his public ministry: that the Gospels and Christian faith are meant, first of all, to be good news for the poor. Any preaching, ministry, or religious activity that is not good news for the poor is not the Gospel of Jesus. As we age, as we mature as Elders, as Sophias, the air we exhale needs to carry always the prophetic message that we are on the side of the poor, and so is God. Moreover, we also need to have the wisdom and the prudence to know when to speak out publicly, when to demonstrate publicly for a cause, when to risk offending others, and when to park the placard and bring out a basin and a towel in quiet prophecy.

In being prophetic, we will invariably be misunderstood and opposed. All true prophets pay a price, and most often that price is rejection. But this itself invites us to a new level of maturity. It invites us, like Jesus, to weep over Jerusalem. We see Jesus do this in a particularly poignant incident when both his person and his message are misunderstood and rejected by sincere people. His reaction is not the normal human reaction to rejection: anger, distancing, and the gleeful feeling that those who are doing the rejecting will ultimately pay for their stupidity and malice. None of that. Instead, Jesus weeps tears of empathy and compassion, the tears of someone who dearly loves someone else but is helpless in preventing that person from hurting herself. Nature and God's intent is that the aging process brings us to this kind of empathy.

Radiating God's Compassion

One of the most challenging and far-reaching lines in the Gospels is Jesus's challenge to us to be compassionate in the same manner that God is compassionate. How is God compassionate? Jesus defines it this way: God's love, he tells us, is indiscriminate; it simply embraces everything. God lets the sun shine on the bad as well as the good, as it shines unselectively on vegetables and weeds alike.

That's a stunning truth. It means God loves us when we are good, and God loves us when we are bad. God loves the saints in heaven and the devils in hell equally. They just respond differently. The father loves both the prodigal son and the older brother, one in his weakness and the other in his bitterness, and his embrace is not contingent upon their conversion. He loves them even in their distance from him.

That is what we are asked to do as Elders: radiate this kind of nondiscriminatory love. That raises certain concerns, of course. How do we let our love shine on the bad as well as the good without saying that nothing matters, that it is okay to live in any way and do anything? How do we love as God loves and still hold true to who we are and what our values are? These are questions whose answers lie right inside the inner dynamics of love itself. When we are being loved, we know intuitively whether that love is blessing our behavior or is there despite our behavior. Young children, being loved by their parents, instinctually know the difference.

Altruistic love embraces in such a way that the recipient knows the difference between being loved and being affirmed in his actions or being loved and not affirmed. Young children experience this all the time from loving parents. But that question is not what is central here.

What is most important here is this: The aging process is designed by God and nature to bring us to the kind of maturity that will radiate God's nondiscriminatory compassion to everyone in the world. As Elders, we are asked to shine our love and compassion on everyone: Christians, Jews, Muslims, Buddhists, Hindus, pagans, atheists, Catholics, Protestants, Evangelicals, Unitarians, New Agers, pro-lifers, pro-choicers, liberals, conservatives, and people of every political and ideological persuasion, as well as people whose views on marriage, sexuality, and aesthetics oppose our own.

There is a time to stand up for what we believe in, to be prophetic, to draw a line in the sand, to point out differences and the consequences of them, and to stand in strong opposition to values

and forces that threaten what we hold dear. But there is also a
time when the heart of an Elder can love everyone, across differences. There is a time to be compassionate as God is compassionate, to let our sun shine indiscriminately on both the vegetables
and the weeds without denying which is which. The aging process is a natural school of charity, of love, to help bring us to this
level of compassion.

Working at Rescuing God from Narrowness

For fifteen years, I taught a seminary course entitled The Theology of God. The students were predominately seminarians preparing for ministry, along with a number of lay students who
were preparing to serve as ministers in various capacities in
their churches. I always taught what the curriculum called for—
namely, how God is revealed in Scripture, how that revelation
has been treated historically by our churches and our theologians,
and how all that has played out in the lives of believers. But my
overriding emphasis, the leitmotif, was always this: *Whatever else
you do in your pastoral practice and preaching, try not to make God
look stupid!*

I tried to impress on them that nothing is as important in our
teaching, preaching, and pastoral activities as the notion we convey of the God who underwrites it all. Every homily we preach,
every catechetical or sacramental teaching we give, and every pastoral practice we engage in reflects the God who undergirds it. If
our teaching is narrow and petty, we make God look narrow and
petty. If our pastoral practice lacks understanding and compassion, we make it seem as though God lacks understanding and
compassion. If we are legalistic, we make God appear legalistic. If
we are tribal, nationalistic, or racist, we make God seem tribal,
nationalistic, and racist. If we do things that befuddle common
sense, we make God out to be the enemy of common sense.

Crassly stated, when we do stupid things in our ministry, we make God look stupid.

This isn't a challenge just for people in ministry. It's a challenge for everyone who is a believer. We always need to work at rescuing God from arbitrariness, narrowness, legalism, rigidity, racism, tribalism, nationalism, and anything else that, through us, gets associated with God. Anything we do in the name of God reflects God.

Atheism, anticlericalism, and most of the negativity leveled against the church and religion today can be attributed to some bad theology or church practice. Atheism is always a parasite, feeding off bad religion. So, too, is most of the negativity toward religion and churches that is prevalent today. Anti-religious attitudes feed on bad religion, and those of us who are religious and churchgoers need to scrutinize ourselves in the light of those criticisms.

We need the honesty to admit that we have seriously hurt many people by the rigidity of certain attitudes and pastoral practices that do not reflect a God of understanding, compassion, and intelligence but instead suggest that God is arbitrary, legalistic, and unintelligent.

I say this in sympathy. It's not easy to reflect God adequately, but we must try to better reflect God, whom Jesus incarnated. What are the marks of God? First, God has no favorites. No one person, race, gender, or nation is more favored than others by God. All are privileged. God is also clear that it's not only those who profess God and religion explicitly who are persons of faith but also those who, regardless of their explicit faith or church practice, do the will of God on earth.

Next, God is scandalously understanding and compassionate, especially toward the weak and sinners. God is willing to sit down with sinners without first asking them to clean up their lives.

Moreover, God asks us to be compassionate in the same way to both sinners and saints and to love them equally. God does not have preferential love for the virtuous.

In addition, God is critical of those who, whatever their sincerity, try to block access to God. God is never defensive, but surrenders himself to death rather than defend himself, never meets hatred with hatred, and dies loving and forgiving those who are killing him.

Finally, and centrally, God is good news for the poor. Any preaching in God's name that isn't good news for the poor is not the Gospel.

Those are the attributes of God, whom Jesus incarnated, and we need to work always at rescuing God from narrowness, even as we are sensitive to proper boundaries and the demands of orthodox teaching. Otherwise, God looks arbitrary, tribal, cruel, and antithetical to love. Christianity, as Marilynne Robinson says, is "too great a narrative to be ... overwritten by any lesser human tale," and that should forbid its being subordinated to narrowness, legalism, lack of compassion, and lack of common sense.

What is the task of an Elder? What wisdom should Sophia be imparting? Perhaps more central than anything else, the task of an Elder is to teach, not least by the very way he is living, that God is credible, trustworthy, compassionate, and loving—and not stupid! The aging process, as a natural monastery, a school of charity, a cauldron that boils out the nonessentials, is wonderfully designed to purify our notion of God, which then becomes one of the gifts we take to the world.

Blessing the Young and Bringing God's Smile to the World

The word *blessing* has become so embedded in our religious language that we can miss its importance anthropologically. How do we bless someone? What does a blessing mean? Simply put, being blessed by others is what frees us from the constricting afterbirth that remains on us sometimes long into adulthood. For example, many is the psychologist or anthropologist who will say that the longing for a father's blessing is the deepest hunger among men in the world today. There is a constriction inside us that only a blessing can take away.

What is a blessing? Anthropologists tell us that there are three components to a blessing: We bless others when we *see them, speak well of them,* and *give away some of our lives for them.* What does that translate to in actual life? Rather than give a full development on this (which I have done in previous writings), let me try to illustrate this with just one example that can serve as a prime analogate for understanding this.

We often see a blessing in a wonderful and pure form in the relationship grandparents have with their grandchildren. The love grandparents have for their grandchildren is surely the purest form of love in this world. In virtually all other relationships, including with a spouse and children, there is (no matter how mature we are) always some degree of self-interest and self-protection. We cannot give the other the pure gaze of admiration. But the pure gaze of admiration is precisely what we often see in the relationship of a grandparent to a grandchild. A grandparent has just the right degree of intimacy and just the right degree of distance to be able to look at the grandchild and spontaneously bless her—that is, see her; admire her life, energy, and beauty without a trace of self-interest; and, without considering the cost, be willing to give up anything for her life, well-being, and joy. A loving grandparent's gaze is one of pure admiration, and its effect on the child is incalculable in terms of helping her develop a healthy self-image in which she feels free and not shamed in her natural energies. The payoff is also for the grandparent. Being a grandparent is not only the purest experience of love on this planet but also the most joyous.

Dare I say this? The most mature expression of sexuality on this planet is not a couple making perfect love, wonderful and sacred though that is. Rather, it is a grandparent looking at a grandchild with a love that is purer and more selfless than any love he has ever experienced, a love without any self-interest, which is only admiration, selflessness, and delight. In that moment, this person is mirroring God looking at the initial creation and exclaiming, "It is good; it is very good!" What follows, then, is that this person, like God, will try to open paths, even at the cost of death, so that another's life may flourish.

A true Elder, a genuine Sophia, is an archetypal grandparent, not just to her own grandchildren but to everyone who is young. I often assert that the penultimate invitation in maturity is to help carry tension for the young. What is the ultimate invitation in maturity? *To bring God's smile to the world.*

There is a deep intention in the aging process. What is its endgame? To make us all, whether we have grandchildren of our own or not, smiling grandparents, seeing the young in their energy and beauty, and giving what's left in our own lives for the betterment of theirs.

Giving Up on Fear

A friend of mine shares this story: He was an only child, and when he was in his late twenties, still single, building a successful career, and living in the same city as his parents, his father died, leaving his mother widowed. His mother had centered her life on her family and was understandably devastated. Her world collapsed; she'd lost her husband, but she still had her son.

The next years were not easy on that son. His mother had little left in her life save him, and he felt a heavy responsibility toward her. She lived for his visits. He spent his days off and his vacations with her, and it was a burden. It prevented him from having the social life and relational freedom he yearned for and from making career decisions he would otherwise have made. He had to take care of his mother and be there for her. As one can guess, their times together were often a burdensome duty for the son. But he did it faithfully, year after year. There was no one else his mother could lean on.

Eventually, as his mother's health began to decline, she sold her house and moved into a complex for seniors. On most of his days off, the son would pick up his mother, take her for a drive in the country, and then take her to dinner before dropping her back at her apartment. One day on such an outing, as they drove along a country road, his mother broke the silence with words that both surprised him and, for the first time in a long time, had his full attention. She shared words to this effect: "Something huge has happened in my life. *I've given up on fear.* All my life I have been afraid of everything—of not measuring up, of not being good enough, of being boring, of being excluded, of being alone, of ending up alone, of ending up without any money or a place to live, of people talking about me behind my back. I've been afraid of my own shadow. Well, I have given up on fear. I've lost everything—my husband, my place in society, my home, my physical looks, my health, my teeth, and my dignity. I have nothing left to lose anymore, and do you know something? It's good. I'm not afraid of anything anymore. I feel free in a way I have never felt before. I've given up on fear."

For the first time in a long time, the son began to listen closely to what his mother was saying. He also sensed something new in her—a new strength and a wisdom from which he wished to drink. The next time he took her for a drive, he said to her, "Mom, teach me how not to be afraid." She lived for two more years, and during that time he took her for drives in the country and for lunches and dinners together, and he drew something from her, from that new strength, that he had not been able to draw before. When she eventually died and he lost her earthly presence, he could only describe what she had given him in those final years by using biblical terms: "My mother gave birth to me twice, once from below and once from above."

Among other things, the aging process is designed to take us to a place where we can give up on fear. As we lose more and more of our health, our importance in the world, our physical attractiveness, our loved ones to death, and our dignity, we have less and less to lose—and less and less to be afraid of. It is one of nature's last gifts to us, and living in a way that others see this new freedom in us can also be one of our last great gifts to those we leave behind.

In the Bible, we are invited 365 times to "be not afraid." It is hard to take up that invitation, but the aging process can take us there. And, once there, we can be the kind of Elder who can help others also take up the invitation.

Proactively Preparing to Move to a Place Beyond the Illusion of Self-Sufficiency, the Beggar's Hut

A number of years ago, I attended the funeral of a man who died at the age of ninety. From every indication, he had been a good man, solidly religious, the father of a large family, a man respected in the community, and a man with a generous heart. However, he had also been a strong man, a gifted man, a natural leader, someone to whom a group would naturally look to take the reins. Hence, he held a number of prominent positions in the community. He was a man very much in charge.

One of his sons, a Catholic priest, gave the homily at his funeral. He began with these words: "Scripture tells us that the sum of a man's life is seventy years—eighty for those who are strong. Now, our dad lived for ninety years. Why the extra twenty years? Well, it's no mystery. He was too strong and too much in charge of things to die at seventy or eighty. It took God an extra twenty years to mellow him out. And it worked. The last ten years of his life were years of massive diminishment. His wife died, and he never got over that. He had a stroke, which put him into assisted living, and that was a massive blow to him. Then he spent the last years of his life having others help take care of his basic bodily needs. For a man like him, that was humbling.

"But this was the effect of all that: It mellowed him. In those last years, whenever you visited him, he would take your hand and say, 'Help me.' He hadn't been able to say those words since he was five years old and still needed help to tie his shoelaces. By the time he died, he was ready. When he met Jesus and Saint Peter on the other side, I'm sure he simply reached for a hand and said, 'Help me.' Ten and twenty years ago, he would, I'm sure, have given Jesus and Peter some advice as to how they might run the pearly gates more efficiently."

That's a parable that speaks deeply and directly about a place we must all eventually come to, either through proactive choice or by submission to circumstance. We all must eventually come to a place where we accept that we are not self-sufficient, that we need help, that we need others, that we need community, that we need grace, that we need God.

Why is that so important? Because we are not God, and we become wise and more loving when we realize and accept that. Classical Christian theologians define God as *self-sufficient being* and highlight that God alone has no need of anything beyond himself. Everything else, everything that is not God, is defined as *contingent,* as not self-sufficient, as needing something beyond itself to bring it into existence and to keep it in existence every second of its being.

That can sound like abstract theology, but ironically it's little children who have an awareness of this. They know that they cannot provide for themselves and that all comes to them as gift. They know they need help. However, not long after they learn to tie their own shoelaces, this awareness begins to fade. As they grow into adolescence and then adulthood, particularly if they are healthy, strong, and successful, they begin to live with the illusion of self-sufficiency: I provide for myself!

It's an illusion, the greatest of all illusions. None of us will enter deeply into community as long as we nurse the illusion of self-sufficiency, as long as we are still saying, "I don't need others! I choose who and what I let into my life!"

G. K. Chesterton once quipped that familiarity is "the greatest of all illusions." He's right, and what we are most familiar with is taking care of ourselves and believing that we are sufficient unto ourselves. As we know, this serves us well in terms of getting ahead in this life. However, fortunate for us, though painful, God and nature are always conspiring together to teach us that we are not self-sufficient. The process of maturing, aging, and eventually dying is designed to teach us, whether we welcome the lesson or not, that we are not in charge, that self-sufficiency is an illusion. Eventually for all of us, there will come a day when, as it was before we could tie our own shoelaces, we will have to reach out for a hand and say, "Help me."

The philosopher Eric Mascall said we are neither wise nor mature as long as we take life for granted. We become wise and mature precisely when we take it *as granted*—by God, by others, by love. We become wise Elders when we recognize this and begin to live it out in our lives.

ALL IN FUNCTION OF FINDING A BEGGAR'S HUT

What do God and nature intend in the stage of our lives between initial retirement and frail old age? What is to be learned in what Hinduism calls the stage of Forest Dwelling? What is the end-game of moving "from role to soul"?

As we articulated in this chapter, these years are meant to engender a new kind of generativity in our lives. Aging and more marginalized, we breathe a new type of generative oxygen into the world, one that not only helps us move from role to soul but also helps the world, particularly the young, know more deeply the reality of soul.

This is a season in our lives that is immensely important in terms of what we bring to others. The aging process is meant to break our illusion of self-sufficiency, humble our egos, and let our souls break through so that we begin to search for a beggar's hut. From there our new task will be to give our deaths away, whereas, up to now, we have been trying to give our lives away.

SEVEN

||||||||||||||||||||||||||||||||

Finding a Beggar's Hut and Giving Our Deaths Away

A whole lifetime is needed to learn how to live, and—
perhaps you'll find this more surprising—a whole lifetime is needed to learn how to die.

TOWARD A SPIRITUALITY OF GIVING OUR DEATHS AWAY

We have a fairly clear notion as to what it means to give our lives
away. But how do we give our deaths away? One way to begin to
answer that question is to look at a number of recent books written by people who were dying of terminal diseases and wrote
memoirs in the hope that their stories would help others find insight and courage in the face of their own mortality. I single out
for special mention the memoirs of Nikos Kazantzakis, Paul
Kalanithi, Bieke Vandekerckhove, Cardinal Joseph Bernardin,
Michael Paul Gallagher, Daniel O'Leary, and Nina Riggs, each of
whom shares how he or she faced a terminal diagnosis. As well,
Parker Palmer, Morris West, Joan Chittister, and Bill Cain have

written deeply insightful works that speak to how we might give our deaths away. And from a purely secular perspective, Katie Roiphe and Erica Jong offer some insightful thoughts on facing one's death in a meaningful way. Each of these writers, I believe, offers something helpful as to how we can face our own deaths in a way that is more noble for us and more life-giving for others.

However, I want to zero in on three people who have been the most helpful for me in trying to find foundational concepts on which to articulate a more structured spirituality of aging and dying. They are Jesus, John of the Cross, and Henri Nouwen.

Jesus on Giving Our Deaths Away

Chapter 4 attempted to explain the difference between how Jesus gave his life for us and how, in a separate act, he gave his death for us: He gave his life for us through his actions. But he gave his death for us through what he couldn't do for us, through what he could only surrender to and absorb—namely, his helplessness, his humiliations, his *passivities*. Because of how hallowed his passivities and helplessness were, the Gospels tell us that blood and water, energy and healing, kept flowing out of his body after he was dead, bringing life and forgiveness to those who knew him. In that blood and water that he left behind, he gave us a final gift, the gift of peace.

In his farewell speech in John's Gospel, Jesus tells us that he is going away but that he will leave us a parting gift, the gift of his peace, and that we will experience this gift in the spirit he leaves behind. How does this work? How does anyone leave peace and a spirit behind?

This isn't something abstract but something we actually experience (perhaps only unconsciously) in our relationships. Each of us brings a certain energy into every relationship we have, and when we walk into a room, that energy in some way affects what everyone else in the room is feeling. Moreover, it stays with them after we leave. We leave a spirit behind us.

For example, if I enter a room and my presence radiates positive energy, trust, stability, gratitude, concern for others, joy in living, wit, and humor, that energy will affect everyone in the room and will remain with them after I have left as the spirit that I left behind. Conversely, if my presence radiates negative energy, anger, jealousy, bitterness, lying, or chaos, everyone will sense that, and that negative energy will remain with them after I have left, coloring what I left behind.

Sigmund Freud once suggested that we understand things most clearly when we see them broken, and that is true here. We see this writ large, for instance, in how a long-term alcoholic parent affects his children. Despite trying not to, he will invariably bring a certain instability, distrust, and chaos into his family, and it will stay there after he is gone, as the spirit he leaves behind, in both the short-term and the long-term.

The opposite is also true. Often, until later, we do not sense the real gift that people who carry a positive energy, stability, and trust into a room bring and what that gift does for us. Mostly it is felt as an unspoken energy, not consciously perceived, and only later in our lives (often long after the people who did that for us are gone) do we recognize and consciously appreciate what their presence did for us. This is true for me when I think back on the safety and stability of the home that my parents provided for me. As a child, I sometimes longed for more exciting parents and naïvely felt safety and stability more as boredom than as a gift. Years later, long after I had left home and learned from others how starved for safety and stability they were as kids, I recognized the great gift my parents had given me. Whatever their human shortcomings, they provided my siblings and me with a stable and safe place in which to grow up. They died while we were still young, but they left us the gift of peace. I suspect the same is true for many of you.

This dynamic (wherein we bring either stability or chaos into a room) is something that daily colors every relationship we have, and it is particularly true regarding the spirit we will leave behind when we die. Death clarifies things, washes things clean, especially regarding how we are remembered and how our legacy affects our loved ones. When someone close to us dies, our relationship with her will eventually wash clean and we will know exactly the gift or burden that she was in our lives. It may take some time, perhaps months, perhaps years, but we will eventually receive the spirit she left behind with clarity and know it as gift or burden.

And so we need to take seriously the fact that our lives belong not just to us but also to others. Likewise, our deaths belong not only to us but also to our families, our loved ones, and the world. We are meant to give both our lives and our deaths to others as a gift. If this is true, and it is, then our dying is something that will impart either a gift or a burden to those who know us.

To paraphrase Henri Nouwen, if we die with guilt, shame, anger, or bitterness, all of that becomes part of the spirit we leave behind, binding and burdening the lives of our family and friends. Conversely, our dying can be our final gift to them. If we die without anger, reconciled, thankful for those around us, at peace with things, without recrimination, and without making others feel guilty, our going away will be a sadness but not a binding and a burdening. Then the spirit we leave behind, our real legacy, will continue to nourish others with the same warm energy we used to bring into a room.

There is indeed such a thing as a good death, a clean one, a death that, however sad, leaves behind a sense of peace. I have witnessed it many times. Sometimes this is recognized explicitly when someone dies, sometimes unconsciously. It is eventually known clearly by its fruit.

I remember sitting with a man dying of cancer in his midfifties, leaving behind a young family, who said to me, "I don't believe I have an enemy in the world. I have no unfinished business." I heard something similar from a young woman, also dying of cancer and also leaving behind a young family. Her words: "I thought I'd cried all the tears I had, but then yesterday when I saw my youngest daughter, I found out that I had a lot more tears still to cry. But I'm at peace. It's hard, but I have nothing left that I haven't given." And I've been at deathbeds when even though none of this was articulated in words, all of it was clearly conveyed in that loving awkwardness and silence often witnessed around someone who is dying. There is a way of dying that leaves peace behind. Whenever someone dies in this way, he, like Jesus, leaves behind the gift of peace.

I suspect that most everyone reading this has had an experience of grieving the death of a loved one—a parent, spouse, child, or friend—and finding beneath the grief, at least after a time, a warm sense of peace whenever the memory of the loved one surfaced or was evoked. This has been the case for me in relation to my parents. Although their farewells were sad, every memory of them now evokes a warmth. Their farewell gift was the gift of peace.

In trying to understand this, it is important to distinguish between being wanted and being needed. When I lost my parents, I still desperately wanted them (and believed that I still needed them), but I came to realize in the peace that eventually settled upon our family after their deaths that our pain was in still wanting them and not in any longer needing them. In the way they had lived and in the way they died, both what they had done for us and what they had absorbed for us, they had already given us what we needed. There was nothing else we needed from them. Now we just missed them. Despite the sadness of their departure, our relationship was complete. We were at peace.

And that is the challenge for all of us vis-à-vis giving our deaths away: to live in such a way that peace will be our final farewell gift to our families, our loved ones, our faith community, and our world. How do we do that?

Peace, as we know, is more than the simple absence of war and strife. Peace is constituted by two things: harmony and completeness. To be at peace, something has to have an inner consistency so that all its movements are in harmony with one another, and it must also have a completeness so that it is not still aching for something it is missing. Peace is the opposite of internal discord or of longing for something we lack. When we are not at peace, it is because we are experiencing chaos or sensing some unfinished business inside us.

Positively then, what constitutes peace? When Jesus promises peace as his farewell gift, he identifies it with the Holy Spirit; and, as we know, that is the spirit of charity, joy, patience, goodness, long-suffering, fidelity, mildness, and chastity.

How do we leave these behind when we die? Well, death is no different from life. When some people leave anything—a job, a marriage, a family, or a community—they leave chaos behind, a legacy of disharmony, unfinished business, anger, bitterness, jealousy, and division. Their memory is felt always as a cold pain. They are not missed, even as their memory haunts. Some people, on the other hand, leave behind a legacy of harmony and completeness, a spirit of understanding, compassion, affirmation, and unity. These people are missed, but the ache is a warm one, a nurturing one, a happy memory.

Going away in death has that same dynamic. By the way we live and die, we will leave behind either a spirit that perennially unsettles the peace of our loved ones or a spirit that brings warmth every time our memory is evoked. When our memory invokes the latter, then, as was the case with Jesus, "blood and water" will continue to flow from our bodies long after we are dead.

John of the Cross on Giving Our Deaths Away

One of the great classical mystics within the deep wells of Christian spirituality is the sixteenth-century Spanish writer Juan de Yepes Álvarez, better known as John of the Cross. He was born in Spain in 1542 and died in 1591. John, perhaps more than any other author—classical or contemporary—outlines systematically what our last stage in life is meant to effect within us and how it is meant to turn us into holy old fools who can now give our deaths away.

For John, even after we have attained an essential maturity, we still have some major blockages (he calls them veils) that render us somewhat less than fully pure in spirit and that keep us from seeing God, others, ourselves, and the world as they really are. We are partially blocked from seeing things face-to-face by our own metaphysics—that is, by the natural way our faculties work.

In understanding the human person, John leaned on the philosophical anthropology of his time (which is arguably still valid). Following thinkers such as Thomas Aquinas, John believed that we have three natural faculties: *Intellect, Will,* and *Memory.* In popular language, we might translate them as *Head, Heart,* and *Person.*

What are the natural movements of each of these faculties? In essence, by natural instinct they work this way:

- The Head—seeks concepts/pictures/imaginative constructs
- The Will—seeks to possess what it is drawn to
- The Person—seeks control and security

For John, these natural instinctual movements of our head, heart, and person serve us well for a good period of our lives, but eventually they become a blockage to seeing others as they really are. How so? Let me risk a story that might serve to illustrate this.

Some years ago, there was a very popular Broadway play that was later turned into an award-winning movie. Entitled *Children of a Lesser God,* it tells the story of a young woman with a double disability: She was deaf and mute. She was also brilliant and strong-willed and consequently became too much of a challenge for most teachers. However, one day she meets a gifted teacher, a young man whose intelligence and spirit are her equal. He is able to effectively help her relate to the world despite her disabilities. His teaching and guidance lead her out into the world and open her up to life in a way she has never experienced before.

It is also a love story. The woman and her teacher fall in love and for a time bask in its fervor. Given the strength of their love, one would expect that they would live happily ever after—but they don't. After a time, an inchoate tension begins to develop in their relationship. They both feel it, are afraid to express it, and do not understand it. For reasons she does not understand, the woman feels the need to distance herself from him. And, given all he has done for her, she feels guilty about this. He, for his part, cannot understand why she is doing this and cannot help but feel resentment toward her.

The situation grows worse and eventually culminates in their breakup. Their breakup conversation could serve as a textbook explanation of how John of the Cross sees our natural metaphysics as eventually standing in the way of us really seeing one another. She tells him that he has been wonderful and that he has taught her to understand herself, helped her open herself to love, and helped her be free. She tells him that he has been a great teacher and that she feels awful about now needing space from him, considering how much he has given her. However, the pain of her pushing him away has taught him something he didn't know he needed to learn. This, in effect, is his response to her: "I've been a good teacher, but not a great one." Why? Because . . .

- I taught you to understand yourself, but not to understand yourself better than I understand you.
- I taught you how to open yourself for love, but not so far that my love can no longer possess you.
- I taught you how to be free, but not so free that you don't need me anymore.

In writing about this, John states that at a certain point in our lives and our relationships, we need to *learn to understand more by not understanding than by understanding.* That may sound nonsensical, but it's an important paradoxical piece of wisdom. For instance, imagine this: A friend comes up to you and says, "I understand you. I have known you for forty years. I know your family background, your ethnicity, your religious background, your strengths and quirks of personality, and even your Enneagram number and where you land on the Myers-Briggs personality assessment! I understand you perfectly!" Would you feel understood? To the contrary, you would feel violated. Imagine this instead: A friend comes up to you and says, "I have known you for forty years, and you're a mystery to me! You really are your own person!" In this, you would feel understood.

For John of the Cross, an initial purification of our lives takes us into basic maturity. But a second purification (a second "dark night") is eventually needed because even though we are living inside this maturity, after a while the natural instinctual movements of our head, heart, and person (which up to now have served us well, as they did the young couple in *Children of a Lesser God*) will become a blockage to real seeing because we are not seeing others as they really are but only in ways in which they fit our understanding, possessiveness, and security.

For John, we are transformed, purified of this impurity, by a painful dark night in which we are forced to accept that we cannot see others, God, our true selves, and the world face-to-face, as they really are, if they have to fit into our concepts of them, our possessiveness, and our security. Once our heads can no longer picture or imagine something, we begin to relate by faith; once our hearts stop trying to possess what they desire, we begin to relate through charity; and once our persons can no longer control things so as to feel secure, we begin to relate through hope. This purifies our eyesight and lets us see through the eyes of faith, charity, and hope rather than through the eyes of conceptual imagining, possessiveness, and control.

How do we enter this dark night? Most of us will enter it through normal growth, relationships, and circumstance (as did the young man in *Children of a Lesser God*). In life, dark nights will happen, usually through breakdown, heartbreak, sickness, diminishment, marginalization, helplessness, and crises of all kinds that are designed to force us into a deeper maturity. Certain events will eventually lead us to the brink, where our natural instinctual way of knowing, feeling, and acting will no longer function for us. This crisis, this dark night, will, if we let it, transform

INSANE FOR THE LIGHT

us and move us toward the purity of eyesight that is given in faith, charity, and hope.

John, however, also offers us a proactive way of entering into this dark night of the spirit. Although he announces this counsel numerous times, it is always the same. For him, we can enter this purifying dark night proactively by *taking the literal word of Scripture and using it to make decisions in our lives that will precisely have us live beyond our natural conception of things, our natural possessiveness, and our natural tendency to ensure our own security.* Translated, this means that we enter this purification proactively when we actively choose to live in such a way that we are no longer guided by concepts, possessiveness, and security. Like Abraham and Sarah in their later years, we set out not knowing where we are going but trusting in God's word. It's then, finally, that we begin to see others and things as they really are.

And what does that feel like? Initially, it is felt as a pain such as we have never experienced, a crushing emotional darkness. Paradoxically, however, it is felt, at the deeper level, as a strength, as our first true experience of nonfragility. Eventually the feeling of emotional darkness changes and the sharp pain turns into simple dryness, which gives us the feeling of being more solidly grounded. Finally, if we live long enough and God gifts us with this experience, we might even begin to experience intermittent periods of ecstasy (though this is perhaps more the exception than the norm).

For John, the final stage of our lives is meant to bring about this radical purification of our instinctual faculties. The process of aging and dying is designed to move us from seeing through concepts, possessiveness, and security to seeing through faith, charity, and hope. This is what constitutes purity of heart and turns us into holy old fools, beggars, *sannyasins.* And Jesus, as we know, promised that those who are pure of heart will see God. John would add that they will also see one another, give their deaths away, and leave behind the gift of peace.

John spends little time talking about death and dying, other than to affirm that it is our final release from all our restless longings. Like many other mystics, John employs a sexual metaphor to convey how he views dying. He looks forward to death (and even prays for it), fantasizing dying as finally coming to "consummation," our wedding night. In that consummation, we will finally see God, one another, our true selves, and the cosmic world as they really are, face-to-face, naked, pure—and the result will be ecstasy.

Henri Nouwen on Giving Our Deaths Away

Henri Nouwen (1932–1996) is arguably the most popular spiritual writer in the English-speaking world in the past seventy-five years. His books continue to be read across denominational and interfaith lines. Born in Holland, Nouwen spent most of his adult life in the United States, teaching at Notre Dame, Yale, and Harvard, and giving lectures to audiences everywhere in the English-speaking world. At the time of his early death, he was living and ministering at L'Arche Daybreak outside Toronto, Ontario.

Nouwen was one of the first contemporary spiritual writers to take up explicitly the theme of giving our deaths away as our last gift to others. Here, in caption, is how he puts it:

> The main question is not, How much will we still be able to do during the few years we have left to live? but rather, How can we prepare ourselves for our death in such a way that our dying will be a new way for us to send our and God's spirit to those whom we have loved and who have loved us?

How do we do this? As we saw earlier, for Nouwen, we do this by living in such a way that when we die, we leave behind a spirit of peace as our legacy. If we die in guilt, anger, and bitterness, not fully reconciled with those around us, our memory will not bring warmth, and our spirit will burden our families and those who knew us. On the other hand, if we die at peace with others, with ourselves, and with God, our memory will evoke warmth in others and leave them with a feeling of peace.

Henri Nouwen wrote more than fifty books, covering virtually every area of spirituality. However, the essence of his spirituality might be synthesized around this structure: twelve major invitations to enter into a way of life wherein we can give our lives and our deaths away as a gift to others. These twelve invitations encourage us to move from one way of living to another:

1. From loneliness to solitude

2. From hostility to hospitality (from *paranoia* to *metanoia*)

3. From fantasy to prayer

4. From relevance to contemplation

5. From willpower to grace

6. From individuality to compassion

7. From impatience to waiting

8. From Christ to Jesus

9. From complexity to simplicity

10. From our wounds being a liability to our becoming wounded healers

11. From giving our lives away to giving our deaths away

12. From our inability to accept love to our acceptance that we are the beloved

It is not within the scope of this book to go into detail on each of these movements. For our purposes, one point needs to be highlighted. Notice in this list that giving our deaths away is not the final movement. Why not? Because there is still a final movement upon which our ability to give our deaths away is predicated: We need to accept radically that we are loved and are God's beloved.

What is at stake here might best be explained through Nouwen's personal story. From the time Nouwen first began to minister, teach, and write, he was extremely popular, much admired, and, in fact, often adulated. From every outward indication, he was a much-loved man. But, for reasons his biographers are still trying to discern, he was mostly unable to take in that love. He spoke and wrote constantly about his loneliness, his feelings of isolation, and his need for love and affirmation—even as he appeared to be living in a sea of love and affirmation. He was a popular professor at both Yale and Harvard, and yet a lack of feeling loved drove him from both places. Eventually, at Daybreak, living among men and women with severe mental disabilities who had never read his books and didn't know he was famous, he felt loved and affirmed in a new way, though still not in a way that fully assuaged his deep wound.

Then, several years before he died, he was struck by a van and was for a time in a deep coma hovering between life and death. While in that coma, he had an experience of feeling loved by God, which radically changed his life. His wound was essentially healed; he now knew he was loved and was God's beloved.

His writings during the last years of his life reiterate again and again that we are God's beloved and that, because we can receive love, we can truly give our lives and our deaths away.

Some spiritual writers suggest that all of Jesus's invitations can be put into one singular invitation: *surrender.* Nouwen would agree, save that he would define that surrender as (finally) letting ourselves be loved. However, as both his books and his life make plain, that is not as easy a task as we might naïvely think. It is not easy to understand love or what our resistances to it are. A brilliant exposé of this is given by the renowned novelist and preacher Frederick Buechner in his book *The Magnificent Defeat.* He wrote an insightful commentary on the biblical passage of Jacob wrestling with a stranger for a whole night. Only in the morning, after he has been defeated, does he realize he was unknowingly wrestling with God.

Jacob is alone one night when a stranger leaps on him. The two end up wrestling silently throughout the entire night. Just as dawn is breaking and it seems Jacob might win, everything is suddenly reversed. With an infinitely superior strength that he seems to have deliberately held back until then, the stranger touches Jacob's hip and renders him helpless. Something deeply transformative happens to Jacob in that experience of helplessness. Now that he knows he is finally defeated, he no longer wants to be free of the stranger's grasp; instead, he clings fiercely to his former foe like a drowning man.

Buechner comments,

The darkness has faded just enough so that for the first time he can dimly see his opponent's face. And what he sees is something more terrible than the face of death— the face of love. It is vast and strong, half ruined with suffering and fierce with joy, the face a man flees down

all the darkness of his days until at last he cries out, 'I will
not let you go, unless you bless me!' Not a blessing that he
can have now by the strength of his cunning or the force
of his will, but a blessing that he can have only as a gift.

This is what Nouwen sees as our lifelong struggle to let ourselves be loved. The blessing for which we are forever wrestling
can come to us only as a gift, not as something we can snatch
through our own talent, through success, through writing sixty
books, through being adulated, or through teaching at Yale or
Harvard. When we are doing those things, we are unconsciously
struggling with something we feel we need to overcome. Eventually after years of struggle, if we are graced, we have an
awakening—often through a crippling defeat. And in the light of
that defeat, we finally see that what we struggled with all those
years was not someone or something to be overcome but the very
love we were resisting and in unconscious ways fighting against.

CONCLUDING PERSPECTIVES

Writing Our Own Obituaries

There comes a time in our lives when we need to stop writing our
own agendas and begin to write our own obituaries. There's a
custom in Judaism for adults to make a spiritual will each year.
Originally, this was more similar to the will we typically make,
where the focus is on burial instructions, who gets what when we
die, and how to legally and practically tie up the unfinished details of our lives. Through time, however, this evolved, and today
this will is focused more on reviewing one's life, highlighting
what's been most precious, honestly expressing regrets and apolo-
gies, and blessing, by name, people to whom the person wants to

say a special goodbye. The will is reviewed and renewed each year so that it is always current, and it is read aloud at the person's funeral as the final words she wants to leave for her loved ones.

This can be a very helpful exercise for each of us, except that such a will is done not in a lawyer's office but in prayer, perhaps with a spiritual director, counselor, or confessor helping us. Practically, what might go into a spiritual will? It focuses on three questions:

1. *What did God want me to do in my life? Did I do it?* All of us have some sense of having a vocation, of having a purpose for being in this world, of having been given some task to fulfill in life. Perhaps we might be only dimly aware of this, but, at some level of soul, all of us sense a certain duty and purpose. The first task in a spiritual will is to try to come to grips with that. What did God want me to do in this life? How well or poorly have I been doing it?

2. *To whom do I need to say, "I'm sorry"? What are my regrets?* Just as others have hurt us, we have hurt others. Unless we die very young, all of us will have made mistakes, hurt others, and done things we regret. A spiritual will is meant to address this with searing honesty and deep contrition. We are never more bighearted, noble, prayerful, and deserving of respect than when we are down on our knees sincerely recognizing our weaknesses, apologizing, and asking where we need to make amends.

3. *Who, by name, do I want to bless before I die and gift with some special oxygen?* We are most like God (infusing divine energy into life) when we are admiring others,

affirming them, and offering them whatever we can from our own lives as a help to them in theirs. Ideally our task is to do this for everyone, but we cannot do this for everyone individually by name. In a spiritual will, we are given the chance to name those people we most want to bless. When the prophet Elijah was dying, his servant, Elisha, begged him to leave him "a double share" of his spirit. When we die, we're meant to leave our spirits behind as sustenance for everyone, but there are some people whom we want to name, to whom we want to leave a double share. In this will, we name those people.

As we affirmed earlier, the four most important things we need to say to our loved ones before we die are *"Please forgive me," "I forgive you," "Thank you,"* and *"I love you."* However, given the tensions, wounds, heartaches, and ups and downs in our relationships, even with those we love dearly, it isn't always easy (or sometimes even existentially possible) to say those words clearly, without equivocation. A spiritual will gives us the chance to say them from a place we can create, which is beyond the tensions that generally cloud our relationships and prevent us from speaking clearly, so that at our funeral, after the eulogy, we will have no unfinished business with those we have left behind.

Some Beautiful Stoics

There is also a rich literature on giving our deaths away that comes to us from outside an explicit faith perspective. What these authors all have in common is that they look at life's deepest questions and face those questions with courage and sensitivity from an agnostic and stoic perspective. How do you make sense of things if there's no God? How do you face the finality of death if there's no afterlife? How do you ground love as an absolute if there's no Absolute on which to ground it? How can the precious events of our lives have lasting meaning if there's no personal immortality? How do we face the shortcomings of our lives and our own mortality if this life is all there is?

These authors face these questions honestly and courageously without an explicit belief in God. They come to peace with them, find meaning for themselves, and garner the insight and courage they need to live and die with answers that don't include faith in God and belief in an afterlife. There's a courageous stoicism in that for sure, but in many of their writings there's also a certain beauty. One gets the sense that this is an honest, beautiful soul wrestling with life's deepest questions and coming to an acceptable peace that itself encapsulates the kind of compassion that all the great religions place at their center.

There are far too many of these authors to mention, but here I single out two, each of whom wrote a wonderfully inspirational memoir while dying of cancer.

The first is the Greek writer Nikos Kazantzakis, famous for writing *Zorba the Greek*. In the months when he was facing his death, he wrote his autobiography, *Report to Greco*. This is a great piece of literature, a work of art, and the testimony of a man facing his own death, outside of an explicit faith, with a courage and insight into life that most of us can only envy. The preface of this book could stand alone as one of the greatest greetings a man has ever given to the death he is imminently facing. It begins with these words: "I collect my tools: sight, smell, touch, taste, hearing, intellect. Night has fallen, the day's work is done. I return like a mole to my home, the ground. Not because I am tired and cannot work. I am not tired. But the sun has set."

The second stoic I recommend is Nina Riggs. Dying of cancer in her late thirties, she penned a memoir that is exceptional in its courage, insight, humor, and capacity to make peace with dying young—all outside a perspective of an explicit faith. While undergoing chemotherapy, she was asked by a nurse how she could face her death without an explicit faith. Nina's answer: "I just know it's going to be all right." And that inchoate faith brought her to a place where she was not only able to face her death with an enviable acceptance but also able, even as she was dying, to pen witty and humorous letters to a young friend who was also dying of cancer. Nina Riggs was able to give away her death.

In religious literature, you can meet some beautiful saints. In secular literature, you can meet some beautiful stoics.

A Personal Creed

When Roman Catholics pray the Hail Mary, we end with the words "Now and at the hour of our death, amen." The late Ivan Illich, the Austrian theologian and social critic, occasionally liked to change the ending of this prayer to these words: "And let me not miss the hour of my death, amen."

I took that ending to heart a number of years ago when, after surviving cancer once before, the cancer returned, and my oncologist told me I probably had only thirty more months to live. Initially, that news rocked me to my roots. I sat in prayer in a deep sadness. Eventually I realized I needed a creed to make those last months precious and to ensure that I did not miss the hour of my own death. Here's that creed:

I am going to strive to be as healthy as long as I can.

I am going to strive to be as productive as long as I can.

I am going to make every day and every activity as precious and enjoyable as possible.

I am going to strive to be as gracious, warm, and charitable as possible.

I am going to strive to accept others' love in a deeper way than I have up to now.

I am going to strive to live a more fully "reconciled life." No room for past hurts anymore.

I am going to strive to keep my sense of humor intact.

I am going to strive to be as courageous as I can.

I am going to strive never to look on what I am losing but rather to look always at how wonderful and full my life has been and is.

And I am going to, daily, lay all this at God's feet through prayer.

It has been nearly ten years since that dire diagnosis and, thanks to God and some very good doctors, I am still alive and wonderfully healthy—but still daily praying that creed so as not to miss the hour of my death.

EIGHT

‖‖‖‖‖‖‖‖‖‖‖‖‖‖‖‖‖‖‖‖‖‖

Thoughts on the Afterlife

What no eye has seen, nor ear heard,
nor the human heart conceived,
what God has prepared for those who love him.

Is there life after death? And if so, will we be self-conscious, our
old selves, or will we be in some cosmic impersonal union with all
that is, no longer conscious of our individual selves?

The vast majority of people throughout history have believed
that there is an afterlife, that death is not the end for us. However,
that belief in life beyond death has taken many different forms.
For some, life after death is conceived of as impersonal; namely,
we will continue to be alive but will no longer be aware of our
individual selves. Rather, we will be part of a great impersonal
union with all things—in peace, in harmony, but not self-aware.
For others (Christians, Muslims, and most Jews), the belief is that
we will be fully alive and fully self-aware and will be in either a
place of peace, communion, and ecstasy with God (heaven) or a
place where God is absent and we are in torment (hell).

This belief that we will all end up in heaven or hell, in which we are fully alive and self-conscious, is, I suspect, the explicit or implicit belief of most people, except for large segments of Hindus and Buddhists who believe that after whatever number of reincarnations it takes to purify ourselves sufficiently for union, we will all eventually be in "heaven" (in union with all that is), though we won't be self-aware. Regardless of the particular modality this might take, the majority of people believe in some form of afterlife.

Indeed, today there is an ever-expanding body of literature that tries to empirically document the stories of people who were clinically dead and were brought back to life through medical procedures, and every one of these stories tells of the person meeting life, love, warmth, and loved ones in the other world before being brought back to life. Any one of these stories alone might easily be dismissed, but hundreds of these stories (and the common thread among them) make for a compelling case that there is life—individual life—beyond death.

What form does this take for those of us who are Christian?

THOUGHTS ON HEAVEN

What is heaven like? The Christian Scriptures tell us that it is beyond all imagination:

> *What no eye has seen, nor ear heard,*
> *nor the human heart conceived,*
> *what God has prepared for those who love him.*

That being said, those same Scriptures give us images of how we might envision it. For example, Isaiah suggests that in heaven the wolf will lie down with the lamb, just as the leopard will with the

kid, and the cow and the bear will make friends, even as the lion
eats straw like the ox. Then he fantasizes that there will be a great
banquet of all the best foods and choicest wines, where everyone
will be happily at table with God and one another forever.

Andrew Greeley once folded these images into another image
and suggested that the physical ecstasy and emotional satisfaction
that results from sexual intercourse between two people who are
deeply in love is the best anticipation currently available to us of
our permanent condition in the resurrected state. The resurrection joys, he submits, will be interpersonal, physical, sexual, and
corporate because we will enjoy them with one another.

More than a few people are shocked by this kind of imagery
when it is applied to heaven. However, it is precisely this image,
sexual consummation, that is dominant in the way many of the
great Christian mystics, including John of the Cross and Teresa of
Avila, envisage heaven. There is a similarity between the sexual
imagery of the mystics and the vision of Isaiah. Both are visions of
heaven as wholeness, as consummation, as love without limit, as
all restlessness finally stilled, as final peace, as ecstasy.

Some religions believe that after death our final state will be
one of ecstasy, where we will be in complete harmony with all
that is. But in this great union, we will lose our individual self-
awareness; our private egos will disappear. Christians, Jews, and
Muslims have a different view. They believe that in the ecstasy of
heaven, we will not only be self-aware but also, paradoxically,
have a heightened self-awareness because (as we know from our
experience of love on this side of eternity) the more deeply we are
in love, the more self-aware we become, and vice versa.

Who goes to heaven? In the two thousand years of Christian
history, there has never been much agreement over how narrow
or how wide the gates of heaven are. In some Christian theolo-
gies, the gates of heaven are very narrow, the conditions for entry

are very stringent, and many (perhaps most) people will not get in. For others, the mercy of God is infinite and thus the gates of heaven are very wide. Indeed, there have always been prominent Christian theologians who are universalists, who believe that ultimately everyone will go to heaven. For them, the final triumph of God and of goodness will be when Lucifer himself converts and goes back to heaven and God's unconditional love completely empties hell.

Who is right? God's unconditional love and infinite mercy and Jesus's prodigal forgiveness of sinners suggest that the universalists are probably closer to the truth than are those who believe that most people will not go to heaven. That being said, the teachings of Jesus do contain some nonnegotiable moral and psychological demands that must be met for entry into heaven. The heavenly banquet table can be heavenly only if everyone at the table gets along with everyone else. But, as we will see later, there can be conversion of heart, forgiveness, and reconciliation with others even after death.

THOUGHTS ON HELL

Hell is never a nasty surprise waiting for a happy person. Nor is it necessarily a predictable ending for an unhappy, bitter person. Can a happy, warmhearted person go to hell? Can an unhappy, bitter person go to heaven? That's all contingent upon how we understand hell and how we read the human heart.

A person who is struggling honestly to be happy cannot go to hell, since hell is the antithesis of an honest desire to be happy. Hell is wanting to be distant from love. Anyone who sincerely wants love and happiness will never be condemned to an eternity of alienation, emptiness, bitterness, anger, and hatred (which are what constitute the fires of hell) because *hell is wanting not to be in heaven.* Bluntly stated, there's no one in hell who's sincerely long-ing for another chance to mend things so as to go to heaven. If a person is in hell, it's because that person truly wants to be distant from love.

But can someone really want to be distant from love—God's love and human love?

We can want something and not want it at the same time. That's a common experience. For instance, take a young child who has just been disciplined by his mother. At that moment, the child can bitterly hate his mother, even as at another, deeper level, what he most desperately wants is his mother's embrace. Until his sulk ends, he wants to be distant from his mother, even as his deepest want is to be with his mother. We know the feeling.

Hatred, as we know, is not the opposite of love but simply one modality of love's grieving, and this dynamic perennially plays itself out in the befuddling, complex, paradoxical relationship that millions of us have with God, the church, one another, and love itself. Our wounds are mostly not our own fault but are the result of an abuse, a violation, a betrayal, or some traumatic neg-ligence within the circle of love. However, this doesn't preclude their doing very damaging things to us. When we're wounded in love, then, like a reprimanded, sulking child who wants distance from his mother, we, too, can for a time—perhaps for a lifetime—not want heaven because we feel we've been unfairly treated by it. It's natural for many people to want to be distant from God. The child bullied on the playground who identifies her bullies with the inner circle of "accepted ones" will understandably want to be distant from that circle—or perhaps even do violence against it.

However, that's at one level of soul. At a deeper level, our ultimate longing is still to be inside that circle of love, which at that moment we seemingly hate because we feel we've been un-fairly excluded from it or violated by it. Thus, someone can be very sincere of soul and yet, because of deep wounds to his soul, go through life and then die with a desire to be distant from what he perceives as God, love, and heaven. But we may not make a simplistic judgment here.

We need to distinguish between what at a given moment we *explicitly* want and what, at that same moment, we *implicitly* (really) want. They're often not the same. The reprimanded child seemingly wants distance from his mother, even as at another level he desperately wants intimacy.

Many people want distance from God and churches, even as at another level they don't. But God reads the heart, recognizes the untruth hiding inside a sulk or a pout, and judges accordingly. That's why we shouldn't be too quick to fill up hell with everyone who appears to want distance from love, faith, church, and God. God's love can encompass, empathize with, melt down, and heal that hatred. Our love should too.

Christian hope asks us to believe things that go against our natural instincts and emotions, and one of these is that God's love is so powerful that, just as it did at Jesus's death, it can descend into hell itself and there breathe love and forgiveness into both the most wounded and most hardened of souls. Hope asks us to believe that the final triumph of God's love will be when Lucifer himself converts and returns to heaven, and hell is finally empty.

Fanciful? No. That's Christian hope; it's what many of the great saints believed. Yes, there is a hell, and, given human freedom, it's always a radical possibility for everyone; but, given God's love, perhaps someday it will be completely empty.

However, there is something that can put us in hell, or, more accurately, something we can do to create a hell for ourselves. The Gospels tell us there is a sin that cannot be forgiven, the sin of "blasphemy against the Spirit." How does one blaspheme the Holy Spirit, and why can't this sin be forgiven?

Here's the context in which Jesus warns us about this sin: The religious leaders of Jesus's time believed as a dogma that only someone who came from God could cast out a demon. Jesus had just cast out a demon, but their hatred of him made this a very inconvenient truth for them to swallow. So they chose to deny what they knew to be true, to deny reality. They chose to lie, affirming (even as they knew better) that Jesus had done this by the power of the prince of demons. Initially, Jesus tried to point out the illogic of their position, but they persisted. It was then that he issued his warning about the unforgivable sin against the Holy Spirit.

At that time, he was not accusing them of committing that sin, but he was warning them that the path they were on could lead to that sin. In essence, this is what is at stake: If we tell a lie long enough, eventually we will believe it, and this will warp our consciences so that we begin to see truth as falsehood and falsehood as truth. The sin then becomes unforgivable because we no longer want to be forgiven. God is willing to forgive the sin, but we are unwilling to accept forgiveness because we see sin as good and goodness as sin. Why, in this case, would we want forgiveness?

It's possible to end up in this state, a state where we judge the fruit of the Holy Spirit (love, joy, peace, patience, kindness, generosity, faithfulness, gentleness, and self-control) as false, as being against life, as a malevolent naïveté, and see their opposites as virtue. The first step in moving toward this condition is lying, refusing to acknowledge the truth. The subsequent steps also involve lying—that is, the continued refusal to accept the truth so that eventually we believe our own lies and see them as the truth and the truth as a lie. In essence, that's what constitutes hell.

Hell isn't a place where one is sorrowful, repentant, and begging God for just one more chance to make things right. Nor is hell a nasty surprise waiting for an honest person. If someone is in hell, that person is there in arrogance, pitying people in heaven, seeing heaven as hell, darkness as light, falsehood as truth, evil as goodness, hatred as love, empathy as weakness, arrogance as strength, sanity as insanity, and God as the devil.

This is one of the salient warnings in the Gospels: *Lying is dangerous, the most dangerous of all sins.* And this doesn't just play out in terms of our relationship with God and the Holy Spirit. When we lie, we're not only playing fast and loose with God; we're also playing fast and loose with our own sanity. Our sanity is contingent on what classical theology terms the "Oneness" of God. What this means in ordinary terms is that God is consistent. There are no contradictions inside God, and because of that, reality can always be trusted to be consistent. Our sanity depends on that trust. For instance, should we ever arrive at a day when two plus two no longer equals four, then the very underpinnings of our sanity will be gone; we'll literally be unmoored. Our personal sanity and our social sanity depend on the truth, on us acknowledging the truth, on us telling the truth, and on two plus two forever equaling four.

Prescinding from who goes to heaven and who goes to hell, Jesus's warning not to play fast and easy with the truth is perhaps his most important spiritual and moral warning of all. What is most frightening and unsettling in our world is ultimately not the growing inequality between the rich and the poor, the dangers of climate change, or even the bitter hatred that perennially separates us from one another (awful as these are). Rather, it is our loss of our sense of truth, our facile denial of whatever truths we judge to be inconvenient. Social media, for all the good it has brought, has also created a platform for anyone to make up her own truth and then work at eroding the truths that bind us together and anchor our sanity. We now live in a world where two plus two often no longer equals four. This plays on our very sanity. The truths that anchor our common life are becoming unmoored.

This is evil, clearly, and Jesus alerts us to that by telling us that Satan is preeminently the *Father of Lies.* Lying is the ultimate spiritual, moral, and psychological danger. It is at the root of what Jesus calls the unforgivable sin against the Holy Spirit. Lying, if persisted in long enough, warps our souls—and it is the one thing that can put us in hell.

Martin Luther once said, "Sin boldly!" He meant a lot of things by that, but one thing he certainly meant is that the ultimate spiritual and moral danger is to cover our weaknesses with lies.

THOUGHTS ON REMAINING IN COMMUNION WITH LOVED ONES AFTER THEY HAVE DIED

A psychologist at a conference I attended shared this story: A woman came to see him in considerable distress. Her disquiet had to do with her last conversation with her husband before he died. She shared how they had enjoyed a good marriage for more than thirty years, with never more than a minor quarrel between them. Then one morning they had a disagreement about some trivial thing (she couldn't even remember the substance). Their argument had ended in anger, and he had stomped out the door to go to work. He died of a heart attack later that day before they had a chance to talk again.

What awful luck! Thirty years without an incident of this kind and now this, anger in their last words to each other! The psychologist first, humorously, assured her that the fault all lay on her husband, in his choosing to die at that awkward moment, leaving her with that guilt.

More seriously, he asked her, "If your husband were here

INSANE FOR THE LIGHT

right now, what would you say to him?" She answered that she would apologize and assure him that considering all their years together, this little incident meant nothing, that their love for each other utterly dwarfed that moment. He assured her that her husband was still alive in the communion of saints and was with them right now. Then he said to her, "Why don't you sit in this chair and tell him what you just shared, that your faithful love for each other completely obliterates your last conversation. Indeed, share a laugh over its irony."

A second story: Recently I met with a family whose father had died by suicide twenty years ago. Through the years they had made peace with that, though, like most families who lose a loved one to suicide, some uncomfortable residue remained. They had long since forgiven him, forgiven themselves for any failure on their part, and forgiven God for the unfairness of his death. But something remained unfinished, something they felt but couldn't quite name. I couldn't name it either, but I could suggest a remedy.

I suggested they have a ritual gathering to celebrate their love for him, celebrate the gift that was his life, and work at redeeming the unfortunate manner of his death. I gave them these ideas: Pick a day, perhaps his birthday or even the anniversary of his death. Meet as a family and have a joyous celebration, complete with champagne, wine, and balloons. Share stories about him, highlighting his joyous spirit, his laughter, and the special energy he brought into a room. I reassured them that he would be there with them, that they are still in a communion of life with him, that he is joyous now. I suggested they celebrate that with him and lift away the twenty years of heaviness. I proposed that the absence of this kind of celebration was what still lay unspoken between them and him.

Stories like this might sound fanciful, like wishful thinking, but they stake their ground in solid Christian doctrine rooted in a faith that tells us that we are in living union with one another in the Body of Christ. As Christians, we believe (as a proposition in our creeds) that we are in union with one another in a living body (an organism, not a corporation) and that this union in one body takes in all of us, both the living and the dead. We can communicate with one another, apologize to one another, make amends with one another, and celebrate one another's lives and energy, even after one of us has died.

As Christians, we are invited to pray for the dead. Not surprisingly, certain Christians balk at this, protesting that God doesn't need to be reminded to be merciful and forgiving. They are right, but in the end, that is not the reason we pray for our deceased loved ones. Despite the stock formulaic prayers we generally use, which ask God to be merciful, the real intent of our prayers and ritual celebrations for the dead is to continue to be in a conscious communication of life with them, to finish unfinished business, to apologize to them, to forgive them, to ask them to forgive us, to remain mindful of the special oxygen they breathed into the planet during their lives, and to occasionally share a celebratory glass of wine with them. That's the Christian belief in the communion of saints.

The Gospels tell us that at the instant of Jesus's death, "the tombs also were opened, and many bodies of the saints who had fallen asleep were raised." They go on to tell us that on the morning of the Resurrection, several women came to Jesus's grave to anoint his dead body with embalming spices. But rather than finding his dead body, they found instead an empty grave and two angels who challenged them with words to this effect: "Why are you looking for a live person in a cemetery? He isn't here. He's alive, and you can find him in Galilee." What's being affirmed here?

The Gospels tell us that Jesus's death opened the tombs and emptied graveyards, and they mean just that. For this reason, as Christians, we don't do much in the way of spiritual practices around our cemeteries. Why? Because ultimately we believe all those graves are empty. Our loved ones aren't to be found there. They're with Jesus, in "Galilee."

What is Galilee in terms of a biblical image? In the Gospels, Galilee is more than a place on a map; it's also a place inside the heart. In the Gospels, Galilee is the place where, for the most part, good things happen. It's the place where the disciples first meet Jesus, where they fall in love with him, where they commit themselves to him, and where miracles happen. Galilee is the place where Jesus invites Peter to walk on water. Galilee is the place where the disciples' souls enlarge and thrive.

And Galilee is also a place for our deceased loved ones. In each of their lives, there was a Galilee, a place where their souls were most alive, where their lives radiated the energy and exuberance of the divine. When we look at the life of a loved one who has died, we need to ask these questions: Where was he most alive? What qualities did he uniquely embody and bring into a room? Where did he lift my spirit and make me want to be a better person?

Name those things and we will have named our loved one's Galilee—and we also will have named the Galilee of the Gospels, that place in the heart where Jesus invites us to meet him. That, too, is where we will meet our loved ones in the communion of saints. Don't look for a live person in a cemetery. She's not there; she's in Galilee. Meet her there.

Sometimes I visit the graves of my parents, who died more than fifty years ago. That's a good experience. I feel some grounding in that, some deep rooting that helps center me. But this is not my real contact with them. No, I meet them among the living. I

meet them when, in my own life, I live what was most distinc-
tively them in terms of their love, faith, and virtue. For example,
my mother was a very selfless woman, generous to a fault, always
giving. When I am generous and give of myself as she did, I meet
my mother. She becomes present, alive. At those times, I do not
experience her as dead, as gone. I meet her in Galilee.

It's the same with my father. His great quality was moral in-
tegrity, a unique stubbornness in faith, an uncompromising insis-
tence that one should not give in to even the smallest moral
compromise. I can be his son in situations when I conquer small
and big temptations in my life; then my father is present, alive,
connected, in a vital community of life with me. I am with him in
Galilee.

Less happy, but just as true, the reverse is also the case: At
those times when I am selfish, when I cannot give myself over in
sacrifice, my mother is absent, dead to me. The same with my
father. When I compromise morally, even on a small issue, my
father is not so alive to me. He recedes like the tide. It is not very
helpful to visit his grave at those times.

Moreover, the Galilee of our loved ones can also be found in
our own Galilee. There's a deep place inside the heart—inside
faith, hope, and charity—where everyone, living or deceased,
is met.

Finally, our belief in the communion of saints gives us a second chance, and that is a much-needed consolation. No matter
who we are, we're always inadequate in our relationships. We
can't always be present to our loved ones as we should; we sometimes say things in anger and bitterness that leave deep scars; we
betray trust in all kinds of ways; and mostly we lack the maturity
and self-confidence to express the affirmation we should to our
loved ones. None of us ever fully measures up. When Karl Rahner
says that for everyone, "all symphonies remain unfinished" in this

life, he isn't just meaning that none of us ever fully realizes our dream; he's also referring to the fact that in our most important relationships, none of us ever fully measures up.

At the end of the day, all of us lose loved ones in ways similar to how that woman lost her husband: with unfinished business, with bad timing. There are always things that should have been said and weren't, and there are always things that shouldn't have been said and were.

But that's where our faith comes in. Indeed, we aren't the only ones who come up short. At the time of Jesus's arrest, trial, and death, virtually all his disciples had deserted him. The timing there was also very bad. Good Friday was bad long before it was good. But—and this is the point—as Christians, we believe neither that there will always be happy endings in this life nor that we will always be adequate in life. Rather, we believe that the fullness of life and happiness will come to us through the redemption of what has gone wrong, not least with what has gone wrong because of our own inadequacy and weakness.

G. K. Chesterton once said that Christianity is special because in its belief in the communion of saints, even the dead get a vote. They get more than a vote. They still get to hear what we're saying to them. So if you've lost a loved one in a situation where there was still something unresolved, where there was still tension that needed easing, where you should have been more attentive, or where you feel bad because you didn't adequately express the affirmation and affection that you might have, know that it's not too late. It can still be remedied!

A number of years ago, I attended a large religious education conference in Los Angeles. Its theme was the Resurrection, its logo was the rainbow, and its closing liturgy brought together about six thousand people. At that Eucharist, after communion, when all the hymns had been sung and everything was quiet, a young couple walked to the altar and picked up the microphone. They looked at the thousands who were gathered there and shared this story: The previous year, their twelve-year-old son had died of cancer after a long struggle. Naturally they were devastated. Nothing prepares parents for the death of a child, and nothing on this side of eternity can soften its blow. Nature itself is set up in reverse—children are equipped to bury their parents, tough as that is, but not the other way around. Children are meant to outlive their parents.

In the immediate hours after their son's death, they were sitting with friends in the living room of their home, drinking coffee and attempting to console each other, when their phone rang. It was a neighbor. "Quick, go look out your front door!" he exhorted. "You'll see something unique." They rushed to look, and there, before them, was a rainbow the likes of which they had never seen before in terms of color as well as scope (it extended perfectly without flaw from one horizon to the other).

They were, of course, taken by its beauty and symbolism (rainbows are a symbol of hope and resurrection), but they were even more taken by the clear, unmistakable intuition that it was their son who was putting on this particular show for their benefit. As they watched in awe and in faith, the mother heard her son gently say inside her, "Mom, this is for you! And because it is hard for you to believe it, I will do it again, the same way, for you tomorrow at this same time!" All doubts that this was some trick of their imagination or mere wishful thinking induced by fatigue, sorrow, and longing were erased the next day when, at exactly the same time, the identical rainbow reappeared. Their son was speaking to them, and they, I'm sure, now forever know what it means to believe in the communion of saints.

I believe their story, not just because they appeared to be very balanced people or because they had enough nerve to share this in front of thousands of people, but because what they shared is not something weird, exotic, New Age, or even all that extraordinary. The story they shared is what the doctrine of the communion of saints means when it is taken out of the creedal formula, out of theology texts, and out of the realm of the abstract and put into our actual lives.

THOUGHTS ON GOD'S UNCONDITIONAL LOVE

Several years ago, a young woman I knew attempted suicide. She was twenty-three years old and away from home. Her frightened, concerned family rushed to her side. They brought her home, got her the best medical and psychiatric attention available, and, most importantly, rallied around her, trying in every way to bring her out of suicidal depression.

They weren't successful. Two months later she killed herself. She had descended into a place that no human love, medicine, or psychiatry could penetrate, a private hell beyond human reach.

What hope do we have in a situation like this? Humanly there isn't any. Outside of faith, she is lost to us and we are help-less to reach her. But inside of faith, there is hope, surprising hope. We have a doctrine in our faith that to my mind is singularly the most consoling belief in all religion—namely, the belief that Christ can descend into hell. One of our Christian creeds tells us that Jesus "descended into hell." What does this mean?

We are not always sure. There are various traditions as to its meaning. In one version, perhaps the most common, the explana-tion is that the sin of Adam and Eve closed the gates of heaven and they remained sealed until the death of Jesus. Jesus's death opened them, and Jesus himself, in the time between his death and resurrection, descended into hell (*Sheol,* the underworld), where all the souls who had died since the time of Adam somehow rested. He took them all to heaven. His "descending into hell," in this version of things, refers to his going into the underworld after his death to rescue those souls.

But another understanding suggests that Jesus's descent into hell refers especially to the manner of his death, to the depth of chaos and darkness he had to endure there and to how the depth of love, trust, and forgiveness he revealed inside that darkness manifests a love that can penetrate into any hell that can be created. That's rather abstract to be sure, so allow me an illustration.

In St. Paul's Cathedral in London, England, there is a famous painting by William Holman Hunt that has inspired numerous, less worthy imitations. It is a painting that depicts Jesus outside a door with a lantern, and the picture suggests that we, who are inside that door, must open the door to allow Jesus in; otherwise he will always remain outside. In some of the imitations of that painting, the artists have taken things further: They have placed a knob on the inside of the door but none on the outside, suggesting that Jesus cannot enter our lives unless we open the door to let him in. I remember as a child seeing this image on a holy card and being haunted by it, fearing precisely that one day I might be too hurt, depressed, or otherwise paralyzed to open that door.

But, powerful as this image is, it is belied by the Gospels.

John, in his Gospel, gives us this picture: On the day Jesus rises from the dead, he finds his disciples huddled in fear inside a locked room. Jesus, unlike the imitation versions of William Holman Hunt's great painting, does not stand outside the door knocking, waiting for the disciples to open it. He goes right through the locked doors, stands inside their huddled circle of fear, and breathes out peace to them. He isn't helpless to enter when they are too frightened, depressed, and wounded to open the door for him. He can descend into their hell by going through the doors they have locked because of fear.

That is also true for the various private hells into which we sometimes descend. We can reach a point in our lives where others can no longer reach into our pain and where we are too wounded, frightened, and paralyzed to open the door to let anyone in. Human love can no longer reach us. But Jesus can enter those locked doors, can descend into our hell.

I am sure that when the young woman whose suicide I mentioned woke up on the other side, she found Jesus standing inside her fear and sickness, breathing out peace, love, and forgiveness, just as he did in the darkness and chaos that he descended into in his death. I am sure, too, that she, sensitive young woman that she was, found in his forgiving breath a peace that was for all kinds of reasons denied her in this life.

What is revealed unequivocally in Jesus's life and death is that God loves us unconditionally and that there is no private hell that would cause God to love us less for even one second. Rather, we live with the assurance that God will always look for us, find us, pass through any locked door we have erected, and, once inside, lovingly breathe out peace to still all that is aching, wounded, and not whole.

PART FOUR

||||||||||||||||||||||||||||||||||

A PARADIGM FOR HUMAN AND SPIRITUAL TRANSFORMATION

To reach satisfaction in all
desire satisfaction in nothing.
To come to possess all
desire the possession of nothing.
To arrive at being all
desire to be nothing.
To come to the knowledge of all
desire the knowledge of nothing.

To come to enjoy what you have not
you must go by a way in which you enjoy not.
To come to the knowledge you have not
you must go by a way in which you know not.
To come to the possession you have not
you must go by a way in which you possess not.
To come to be what you are not
you must go by a way in which you are not.

When you delay in something
you cease to rush toward the all.
For to go from the all to the all
you must deny yourself of all in all.
And when you come to the possession of the all
you must possess it without wanting anything.
Because if you desire to have something in all
your treasure in God is not purely your all.

NINE

A Paradigm from a Christian Mystic

First comes falling in love, which is the easy part. Then comes learning to love, which is the hard work. And then there is living in love, which is the best part.

It can be helpful to know a little about John's life and background before looking at his notions of how we mature. As I mentioned earlier, John was born in Spain in 1542, and if Shakespeare's Romeo and Juliet would have had a child, it would have been John of the Cross. There is romance in his origins and his genes. His father came from a family of wealthy silk merchants but fell in love with a peasant girl, and in order to marry her, he had to renounce his family's wealth and privilege. They married and landed in poverty. Moreover, John's father soon fell into bad health and died shortly after the boy's birth, leaving his mother to raise young John on her own. She supported herself and her son by working as a weaver, selling the things she made.

As a young boy, John began working in a local hospital to

help support his mother. We can easily guess what his job en-
tailed, given that these were the days before indoor plumbing
when hospitals used bedpans. However, as he did this job, he was
noticed for his exceptional diligence and obvious intelligence.
One of the administrators at the hospital, sensing something special in John, sent him off to school and paid for his education.
John made the most of it. He was educated by the Jesuits and received a solid formation in the humanities, becoming well-versed
in Greek and the classics. At age twenty, he entered the Carmelite
order and was sent to study at Salamanca, one of the leading
Spanish universities of the time. There he studied arts, philosophy, and theology and was recognized for his brilliance, becoming the prefect of studies while still a student.

He was ordained a priest at age twenty-five and shortly afterward met a Carmelite nun, Teresa of Avila (who would herself
become a famous mystic). This was the age of the Reformation,
and many religious orders, like the church itself, stood in need of
reform. Teresa was trying to reform the women's side of the Carmelite order and asked John whether he would work on reform-
ing the men's side. He agreed.

Soon afterward, under her guidance, he set up a small community he called a house of "strict observance" within the Carmelite order. At this time, he changed his name to Friar John of
the Cross. Since part of their strict observance was to go around
barefoot, they were soon called Discalced Carmelites. As one can
guess, it did not take long before tensions developed between
these reformed Carmelites and those who were against the reform, and John suffered much from the tension. At one point, he
was taken by force by nonreformed members of his order, asked
to renounce the reform, and then imprisoned when he refused to
comply. In prison he was lashed, resulting in wounds that did not

heal properly for years. Indeed, he would have died there had a sympathetic Carmelite brother not helped him to escape.

While imprisoned, he wrote his now-famous poems. After his escape, he fled to southern Spain, where he was safer. While there, he was excommunicated from the church for a period, but he probably didn't hear of this censure. Eventually things settled down and the Discalced Carmelites he had founded became a separate order within the Carmelites. John spent most of his last years as chaplain in the convent in Avila where Teresa lived, becoming her spiritual director. These were years of relative calm when he wrote all his major works. There is an interesting history to his writing: The nuns he was ministering to asked him to explain his poetry, and his commentaries on his poems became the basis for all his books. He died in 1591 at age forty-nine. Beyond the influence of his mystical writings, he is still ranked within Spanish literature as one of its great poets.

John was a genius, a mystic, a romantic, a poet, and an artist. A number of other medieval mystics were similarly gifted. What sets John apart is how he integrated the romantic, the poetic, and the artistic into the intellectual framework he had developed during his extended classical education. He was a mystic-poet who was also a doctor of philosophy, theology, and other academic disciplines of his time. Unlike many mystics whose writings are like beautiful wildflowers in a desert, his writings have a clear intellectual structure. In his writings, we do get the beautiful wildflowers (the poetry, the mystical insight, and the romance), but we get them in a wonderfully synthesized structure that ultimately forms a coherent system within which to understand ourselves.

For John, growing toward initial maturity and then final maturity in our aging is an organic process, an unfolding of life wherein certain circumstances will naturally push us to a new phase. And, in his view, there are *six* stages we pass through on the journey from immaturity to maturity, from selfishness to altruism, from fantasy to reality, and from this life to heaven.

We will briefly describe each stage and then, in more depth, tease out how all this happens in real life.

FIRST STAGE: UNHEALTHY INDIFFERENCE (PRE-CONVERSION)

This stage in our lives has four characteristics: unhealthy indifference, lack of focus, disordered erotic energy, and the pleasure principle as our primary motivation for action.

We feel our erotic energies very deeply but lack clear direction. Love can be, and often is, fairly promiscuous. In contemporary colloquialism, we "hang loose" and love what we are attracted to at the moment, especially what brings pleasure. Choices and commitments are made ultimately on the basis of what gratifies us. At this stage, there is no true commitment, no true virtue, and no real giving of ourselves to anything beyond ourselves. Regardless of how sophisticated and altruistically disguised an action may look, in the end, we are doing our own thing. Narcissism, egoism, and idiosyncratic preference are the basis of our actions.

At this stage, no real prayer, love, or service of others is happening, even though we may be under a powerful illusion that we are genuinely praying, loving, and serving others. For John, this is what immaturity looks like.

SECOND STAGE: FALLING IN LOVE (CONVERSION)

There is a saying that the world can change in fifteen seconds. The novelist Morris West says, "All conversion begins with the act of falling in love." Both are right. Immaturity is ultimately overcome by falling in love because, with that, everything changes and three things begin to characterize our lives: focus, the loss of indifference, and a change in what fuels our motivation.

In brief, transformation begins with falling in love—with a person, with God, or with some principle, ideal, or ideology. With that comes the immediate loss of indifference. There is now a clear focus; we no longer "hang loose." In fact, very often we become obsessed with whom or what we have fallen in love with to the point of losing our freedom. This brings with it, at one level at least, a new motivation. There is an initial movement beyond ourselves, beyond the pleasure principle in its crasser form; we now can be quite self-sacrificing, at least as this serves our beloved. This is the initial movement toward maturity.

THIRD STAGE: THE HONEYMOON (FIRST FERVOR)

Following the initial moment of falling in love, almost invariably a person goes through a season characterized by something John calls *first fervor,* something we might call the honeymoon.

While in the honeymoon stage of love, our lives are colored by intense feelings, passion, a desire for uniqueness, endless energy in areas that pertain to our beloved, public display to the world regarding our beloved, and ease in communicating with our beloved.

How this plays out in life will become clearer through the examples given later. In brief, during this period, we act as one acts when one is on a romantic honeymoon. We feel a passion that relativizes all other loves, past and present; we sense that this love is unique, poetic, special; we believe that nothing is too much for us when it comes to our love; we draw a powerful energy from that love; we are given over to public display (to let the world know that we have found love); and we experience a constant desire to talk to the beloved or, barring that, to talk to others about our love.

FOURTH STAGE: THE DEATH OF THE HONEYMOON (THE WANING OF FERVOR)

All honeymoons eventually end. That is a fact of experience. Experience also teaches how our feelings change when this happens. When our initial fervor dies, it is followed by a certain disillusionment, a loss of passion and desire, and a certain boredom with the one who formerly seemed the answer to our every restless desire. With that comes a certain reticence to talk to or about the loved one. All of this can, and often does, cause confusion in the person. There is a certain disappointment, a feeling of having lost something important, coupled with the desire to do things that will bring back the fervor of the honeymoon.

What causes this change? In some cases, the honeymoon dies because of infidelity and lack of interest; we fall in love with someone else or simply lose interest in the person we once loved so passionately. In such a case, the honeymoon dies not because a heathy transformation is taking place but for the opposite reason—namely, we revert to immaturity. However, in John's view, even if we do remain faithful, our honeymoon will end. All initial fervor eventually dies, and disillusionment, loss of passion, boredom, and loss of discursiveness toward and about one's beloved replace the passion of the honeymoon. Why does this happen even in the most faithful relationships? Because that is the way relationships unfold organically. The honeymoon ends not because nature and God are cruel and want to cut off our passion and pleasure. No. Honeymoons end because, up to this point, we have been more in love with the experience of being in love and in what that experience was doing for us than we have been in love with another person. That is why we experience disillusionment (and note that disillusionment is often a very healthy feeling, since it is the dispelling of an illusion). Honeymoons end so that we can come face-to-face with the person behind the experience. Only after a honeymoon ends do we find out whether we are really interested in somebody or whether we are mostly interested in how relating to that person makes us feel. Hopefully the illustrations given in the next section will help make this clear.

FIFTH STAGE: MATURITY (PROFICIENCY)

This stage has three characteristics that build upon one another: decision, dryness, and ease. We enter maturity when we make a decision for its own sake, as opposed to deciding out of self-interest. This is followed by dryness, a stage in which we feel little or no psychological or emotional consolation in relation to our beloved. However—and this is key—if we persevere in fidelity to that person, we will eventually begin to feel a certain ease and loving attentiveness in our relationship with the one we love. In his presence, we will begin to feel not the passion of the honeymoon but a *deep sense of being at home.*

John calls this stage *proficiency* and sees it as a major development in our human and spiritual journey. At this stage, we are mature, essentially unselfish, giving our lives away. And we can stay in this stage for the rest of our lives—unless we make one final dramatic leap of faith.

SIXTH STAGE: ULTIMATE HUMAN MATURITY
(FINAL PURIFICATION)

For John, relatively few people enter this final stage by choice and even fewer complete it. To enter and complete this stage is to at-

tain the highest degree of maturity possible in this life, full saint-
hood in Christian terminology.

Unlike the previous stages, this one does not unfold naturally,
organically. To enter it, we have to make a proactive decision, a
particularly challenging one. John calls this stage the *dark night of
the spirit*.

It begins when, after long years of living in maturity, a person
makes a *radical decision to live by faith alone*. In essence, a person
enters this stage when she decides to live and act according to the
written dictates of the Christian creeds and Scriptures, even when
this goes bitterly against what her head, heart, friends, common
sense, and conventional wisdom suggest. At this stage, a person
truly radicalizes her discipleship in Christ, and nothing that she
can see, feel, think, touch, taste, or sense alters what she understands is asked of her through the written dictates of Christ and
the church. In a manner of speaking, one becomes a fundamen-
talist. The written word of Scripture speaks to the essence of life
without the usual nuances that come from common sense and
practical wisdom, and it determines our actions and what we believe to be truly wise.

Immediately after a person makes such a decision, the ease of
proficiency dissolves and he enters a period of fierce disconsolate
dryness. For John, this is by far the most painful part of the journey of growth and transformation. In this period, the person is
habitually disconsolate and in interior pain. In Christian terms,
this is the fullest experience of Good Friday given to us in this
life. Paradoxically, however, even as one's outer world is crum-
pling, his inner world is growing more secure. During this period, the type of ease that was felt during the time of proficiency
dissolves into a raging desolation. However, at the deepest level of
his person, a new kind of security is dimly felt.

For John, this raging dryness can last for a long or short time.

Perhaps, too, one may die during it. However, if a person perseveres (and, for John, nobody turns back once she enters this final stage), the dryness eventually gives way to a deep peacefulness and tranquility that bring the return of passion, an overwhelming sense of the goodness of all things and of their beauty, a deep empathic connection with all of reality, and (for some, at least) intermittent ecstasies. In Christian language, this is Easter Sunday.

For John, we enter this stage proactively, purposefully, by making a radical, life-altering decision to live in a way that cuts us off from all former securities. However, even though John does not develop this aspect, one can also enter this stage by compulsion—for example, if one is told by a doctor that he has a terminal illness and will die within a few months. This diagnosis radically and inalterably changes that person's life, and the symptoms that John describes (such as raging desolation) will naturally follow.

THESE, FOR JOHN OF THE Cross, are the *six* stages of growth and transformation. In biblical terms, they constitute a paradigm for how a grain of wheat falls to the ground and dies in order to come to new life. Here is an example of each. The dynamics inherent within this paradigm, as we shall see, work the same through *love, prayer,* or *service,* regardless of where this transformation takes place.

AN ILLUSTRATION OF TRANSFORMATION THROUGH LOVE

Imagine a young man named Joe. Joe is twenty-four years old, has recently graduated from college, and, in terms of his love life, is at the stage of *pre-conversion.* What is Joe like?

He has a lot of erotic energy inside him, but he lacks focus and commitment. He is unhealthily indifferent, a state he euphemistically calls "hanging loose." He loves women but is not committed to any one woman. In his relationships, he is guided by the gratification principle: He is interested only to the extent that there is something in it for him. Moreover, at this stage, he even feels quite smug about himself regarding his relationships with women. His promiscuity is, for him, not a moral issue.

But his world changes in fifteen seconds. One night at a party, he meets Mary. He falls in love. This is the moment of *conversion*. Immediately his indifference dies. His erotic energies focus sharply. He is no longer in love with women; now he is in love with Mary and no longer wants his freedom to play the field. Promiscuity no longer interests him; commitment to Mary does. Concomitant with this, there is a change in his motivation. He, who up until now had thought only of his own pleasure, now becomes (at least in relationship to Mary) quite generous and able to renounce many of his own wants and pleasures for her sake.

Mary also falls in love with Joe, and they marry. For the first months after their marriage, they are in the honeymoon stage of love, *first fervor*. He feels a passion for her and an emotional bond that relativizes anything he has ever felt in a relationship. He fantasizes that their marriage will be one in a million, the most unique love two people have ever shared. The love energizes him and is prone to excess. Also, at this stage, it is important to him to publicly display his love for Mary. They hold hands in public and, through that and other gestures, continually let the outside world know they are in love. Very importantly, during this time, he has both the appetite for and ability to talk with Mary quite easily and endlessly, and when he is not talking to her, he is talking about her. He is infatuated and obsessed with her in a way that makes the indifferent Joe of mere months ago seem an entirely different

person. Naïvely he feels that their love will continue like this forever.

Would that it could, but it does not. Like all honeymoons,
eventually the emotional magic is over. Imperceptibly (though in
some cases this can also happen quite dramatically) the fervor
lessens, and, at some point, Joe becomes disillusioned with Mary.
The disillusionment is not because he no longer sees her as a good
person but because he begins to see her *as just a person.* "Disillusionment" means the breaking of illusion and the coming to reality. After living with Mary for a time, he comes to realize that
despite her goodness and beauty, she is just one person, one
woman—not all of femininity incarnate. Up to this point, he had
his own version of Saint Augustine's famous prayer: "You have
made my heart lonely, Lord, and it was lonely until it rested in
Mary!" In his illusion of her, she was a goddess—femininity and
humanity all in one. She was enough to still his restlessness. Now
he is still lonely, despite Mary. Moreover, beyond this disappointment, he recognizes for the first time that Mary has faults and
blemishes. Thus, his disappointment, in the end, is in both that
she is just a person and that she is not a perfect person.

That double disappointment brings along with it something
he has never experienced in relation to Mary: boredom. At this
point, he also begins to lose some of the fiery passion and emotions he had for Mary. Upsetting for him too (and perhaps even
more so for Mary!) is the fact that he no longer has a ready incli-
nation to talk with Mary. He finds himself often without a lot to
say to her, despite her pleas and his memory of seemingly better
times. However, even as the feelings of the honeymoon are dying,
paradoxically Joe is beginning, in the real sense, to more genuinely care for and be solicitous about Mary. The joyous emotions
of the honeymoon are mostly over, but despite that, he is now
more deeply bonded to Mary.

What has happened here? Why did the honeymoon die? Why do all honeymoons die? Is God a masochist who does not like us to have pleasure for too long?

For John of the Cross, when honeymoons die (providing they die for the right reason and not because of infidelity of some kind), God takes away the passionate feelings to bring us more face-to-face with the person behind those feelings. Joe's honeymoon with Mary had to die because, until now, he has not been in love with Mary. Rather, he has been in love with the experience—in love with being in love, in love with how love made him feel, in love with femininity, in love with the goddess archetype in Mary; in short, he has been in love with many things, *but not in love with Mary*! Now, with the honeymoon feelings gone—after they served to bond him deeply with Mary—he is left looking at Mary as a real person. He must now decide whether he actually loves Mary beyond the honeymoon he has had with her.

John calls this stage of love the *passive night of the senses*. It is a crucial and pivotal stage in relationships. Joe can now turn back. He can leave Mary, find someone else to fall in love with, and try to have another honeymoon. Or he can move to the next stage with Mary and experience *proficiency* in love.

Joe does this. He makes a decision for Mary. He decides that, despite the disillusionment, he will continue in marriage with Mary and work with her in building a relationship. His decision is based on two things: the bond that grew during the period of fervor and his values. He senses that to continue his marriage is *the right thing*, the higher thing to do.

Initially, he experiences a certain dryness in the relationship. He comes home to Mary, even though sometimes it would be more interesting to go elsewhere. He finds it difficult to communicate with her. They both see their honeymoon stage as a certain golden age in their relationship. Occasionally, though unsuccessfully, they try to have a second honeymoon to recapture the emotional magic.

Eventually the dryness becomes ease. Joe still misses the magic of the honeymoon, but what he now experiences with Mary is a deepening sense of being at home. The idea and the feeling of being at home somehow melt in with his idea of Mary. There is still, intermittently, a feeling of restlessness and boredom, but habitually there is the sense of being comfortable, at ease, at home with Mary. Perhaps he and Mary live out their days in this proficient state until one of them dies. Their children and friends sense that their marriage was a very good one.

Or perhaps, after years of praying together, with their children long since grown and self-sufficient, they decide on a very radical option. Perhaps, like Abraham and Sarah, who were asked by God to set out without knowing where they were going, they decide to let the written word of God guide them beyond where they would go if they continued to guide themselves by practical wisdom alone. They decide, in response to the beatitudes, to open their home to street people and become holy beggars in the style of Hindu *sannyasins.*

Initially, after making such a decision, they feel desolation and a raging dryness. The secure sense of *being at home,* which characterized their last years together, breaks down and, with it, all their securities. A painful period of emotional and intellectual confusion and insecurity follows, even as neither turns back on this new radical road they have taken.

They live through this dryness, the most bitter either has ever experienced. Imperceptibly it begins to change, and one day, instead of the dryness and insecurity between them, they begin to feel again a passion stronger than they felt all those years ago when they first fell in love. Moreover, along with these deep and quasi-ecstatic feelings they feel for each other, they begin to feel the same kind of feelings about the world and all other people. They are constantly overwhelmed by the goodness and beauty not just of each other but of the whole world and everyone in it. The emotional magic of their first honeymoon pales in comparison with this new way in which they are inflamed with love.

In Christian terms, their love has now resurrected. It has fallen in the ground, died, and come through "Good Friday," and it is now the kind of love that will grow and last forever. There will be no death of this second honeymoon. There will be only passion, joy, and ecstatic union of life forever. When John of the Cross speaks of going through the dark night of the soul, it is this process he is describing.

AN ILLUSTRATION OF TRANSFORMATION
THROUGH PRAYER

Just as a person can be transformed and brought to maturity through love, so, too, can one mature through prayer. Let us imagine a young woman named Martha. Martha is twenty-four years old, has recently graduated from college, and, in terms of her prayer life, is at the stage of *pre-conversion*. What is Martha like?

She does not have much interest in prayer and most times simply does not pray. In her prayer life, and in her religious life in general, she lacks focus and is unhealthily indifferent. She is guided by the gratification principle in that she prays and attends religious services when there is something in it for her.

One evening, out of boredom and a desire to tag along with her friends, she goes to a charismatic prayer meeting. She has a religious experience and is overcome with both the desire to pray and a facility for it. She is baptized in the spirit and, among other things, begins to speak in tongues. She has fallen in love, experienced *conversion.*

Immediately, not unlike Joe, who has fallen in love with another person, she enters a honeymoon stage, *first fervor.* In prayer, she has intense emotions and is spontaneously moved to tears, deep joy, powerful feelings of empathy for the world, and an intense desire to serve God completely to the point of giving up her life. With that come fantasies of uniqueness and greatness. Martha believes she can be a great saint, a mystic even. In her mind, she will pray and serve God like very few others ever have. Like the young lover, she is full of endless energy and is prone to excess in her prayer life. She goes to a prayer meeting nearly every evening and stays there longer than necessary. It is also important for her, during this time, to display her new love publicly, to let the world know she has found Christ. Her car is covered with bumper stickers: "I Have Found Christ," "Christ Saves," "God Loves You," and so on. Around her neck she wears a cross, and on her lapel is a dove pin. At this time, she has both the appetite and ability for easy conversation with God in prayer. When she is not praying, she is, much to the chagrin of her friends, talking about praying! And, like the young lover, she naïvely believes that this will go on forever.

But it does not. Imperceptibly or perhaps dramatically, things change. There comes a day when the fervor is gone. Her honeymoon in prayer is over. She enters the *passive night of the senses,* the waning of fervor. Like the lover going through this phase, she begins to experience disillusionment, a loss of consolation, boredom, and a loss of both the appetite and capacity for prayer. She becomes disillusioned with her prayer life and often with her prayer group as well. During her time of fervor, she had underlined in bright colors nearly every line in her Bible because it was so meaningful, but now the Bible bores her. She finds herself unable to pray as she did before and feels no passion or emotion in her prayer.

However, if these symptoms are not the result of infidelity or emotional or physical illness, then, even as her fervor is waning, she will experience at a level beyond her emotions and intellect a desire for prayer and solicitousness about God and the things of religion. She will no longer have the magical feelings about prayer that she once had, nor will she have the ability to pray as easily as she used to. But she will want to pray, even as she is unsure about what that now means.

Again, it is useful to insert a reflection at this point. Why did her honeymoon in prayer die? As for the lover, her honeymoon had to die because during her period of fervor, she was not as much interested in God as she was in the experience of praying and how that made her feel. For John, in the passive night of the senses, God dries up the experience so as to give someone a chance to meet more face-to-face the person behind that experience. After the honeymoon had done its work of bonding Martha to God more deeply, God dried up her experience of prayer to give her the opportunity to become interested in God and not just in the experience of praying.

Although she is somewhat confused and disappointed about the death of her fervor, Martha now decides that she will pray not because it feels good but because she is interested in God. She makes a decision for prayer and with that enters *proficiency*.

Initially, she experiences mostly dryness in her prayer. Unable to pray as she formerly did, she spends her prayer time just sitting quietly. Slowly the dryness gives way to a certain ease and comfort. She still has intermittent aridity in her prayer, and her prayer time is not an exciting time, but it is good, a time when she feels centered, at home, and in God's presence.

This can continue for a short or long period. She may even

die during the months or years of proficiency. If she dies, she will die, in John of the Cross's eyes, quite advanced and mature but not yet fully transformed.

However, if she does not die in this phase, she will sense inchoately after some time that God is asking something more radical of her. Like Abraham and Sarah, she will sense that God is now calling her to set out without knowing where she is going. Her prayer life now, in effect, becomes her whole life. She realizes that until this point, she has been partially rationalizing and not giving herself over fully to the demands of the Sermon on the Mount. She decides that from now on she will no longer use her practical vision and the "friendly counsel" of her family and friends to smooth away the sharp edges of the demands of the Sermon on the Mount. She decides to live her life fundamentally in light of those demands.

What this means practically can vary from case to case. Perhaps she runs off and joins Mother Teresa's nuns or becomes a Christian *sannyasin*. Or she gives away all her money and possessions and lives most austerely. As with Joe and Mary, entry into the dark night of the spirit can take many practical forms. Whatever its specific form, it takes place when, after a sufficient time of preparation, a person uses the written word of God to actually guide her in life, beyond the dictates of common sense, practical wisdom, and the measured advice of biblical commentators and spiritual directors who are unfamiliar with this final phase of paschal transformation.

In this case, Martha makes this radical leap of faith. Her family and friends are very upset with her and worry about her. But this is not her greatest pain and insecurity. Rather, almost immediately upon making this decision, she is thrown into desolation. She feels that God has let her down. At times, she has severe doubts about her faith and begins to wonder whether God exists.

The habitual ease and sense of being at home, which she had just recently felt in prayer, disappears. She feels lost, beyond any hope anyone can offer her. That is why she is not interested in the advice of concerned family and friends who suggest things she should do to regain her "old self," to go back on her radical decision and live a "normal" life like everyone else. At this stage, Martha knows that a "normal life" is not an option. Nothing turns her back. She stays with the pain and confusion, knowing that, as the author of Lamentations says, there are times when one can only "put one's mouth to the dust" *and wait*!

She perseveres, and one day it gets better. One day (and this can be after a long time or a short time) the dryness gives way to a passionate fervor, one deeper than what she felt all those years ago at that prayer meeting when she had her religious conversion. This fervor now begins to stir habitually inside her. In it she experiences an overwhelming sense of the reality and graciousness of God, as well as a concomitant sense of the overwhelming goodness and beauty of all creation. She has trouble containing her sense of this goodness and finds herself occasionally in ecstasy.

In John of the Cross's terms, Martha's prayer life has now undergone the dark night of the soul. The seed that was there at her initial conversion has fallen in the ground, died, and brought forth new and eternal life. The feelings she now has will never die. She has moved beyond being interested in herself and the experience of prayer to being interested in God. Good Friday is over. She is now living Easter Sunday.

AN ILLUSTRATION OF TRANSFORMATION THROUGH SERVICE

Some years ago, I knew a young man who, upon graduating from college, had very little, if any, interest in social justice and the poor. He was interested in his forthcoming career, his social circle, sex, travel, and the enjoyment of his youth. In terms of a life of service, he was in the stage of *pre-conversion*. As a graduation gift, his parents gave him several thousand dollars, which he used to go on a six-month tour with friends. Their tour eventually took them to South America, where their chief interest was not the poor but the beaches and the good life.

As we all know, conversion can be most surprising. While in South America, this young man broke away from his tour with his friends for a week to visit a Canadian missionary whose family was neighbors of his own family back home. During that week with his missionary friend, he met the poor, and, like Joe, who fell in love, or Martha, who had a religious experience at a prayer meeting, his life radically changed and something inside him irrevocably shifted. In that moment, he lost his unhealthy indifference and moved beyond the pleasure principle as his natural motivation for acting. In that moment, he experienced *conversion*.

As for Joe and Martha, with that conversion came *first fervor*. He parted with his friends and returned home. Once there, rather than proceed in starting a career, he began to work at the local food bank, lived on virtually nothing, and got involved with numerous groups that were active in social justice activities. He entered the honeymoon stage of his conversion. As he worked with and for the poor, he was inflamed with feelings about them. Like the lover and the religious neophyte, he had fantasies of uniqueness and greatness. In his mind, he would become the world's greatest social worker. Like his counterparts in love and prayer, he, too, at this stage had inexhaustible energy and was prone to excess. He worked endless hours for the poor and spent many of his evenings at meetings discussing projects, protests, and political programs. And, like the young lover and the religious novice, it was important to him to make public display of his commitment. His car was covered with bumper stickers: "Boycott Shell," "Resist the USA in Central America," "God Is a Woman . . . Listen to Her!" His designer clothes hung unworn in his closet, and he wore only khakis and denim. At this time, parallel to those who have had a recent conversion in love or prayer, he had both the appetite and ability for a certain discursiveness. In his case, this took the form of an endless ability to talk to the poor and an equal ability to talk *about* them when he was not talking *to* them. At this time, too, he was under the naïve impression that he would feel this way forever.

He did not. There came a day a few years later when the fervor was gone, the honeymoon over. Perfectly parallel to what happens when the first fervor of love and prayer die, he began to feel in his relationship to the poor a sense of disillusion, a loss of passion, and boredom. His words seemed empty, and he drew little consolation in talking to the poor or in talking to others about them. He preferred to say a lot less. That is the stage my friend is in at present. However, since his commitment to the poor has been genuine, he is still deeply committed to them and genuinely solicitous for them, despite his lack of felt consolation in serving them.

Again, an important question needs to be raised here: Why did the honeymoon die? Why did his fervor dry up? John of the Cross would say that, like the case of the lover and the woman in prayer, God took away all natural consolation in the experience so that this young man might be brought more face-to-face with what is behind the experience, the poor themselves. Until this stage, the *passive night of the senses,* the waning of fervor, he was in love not with the poor but with the experience of serving the poor and with how that made him feel.

I judge my friend to be, right now, in the stage of *proficiency.* He is serving the poor, just as he did while in fervor. His decision

to continue to serve was based not upon the naïve hope that someday he would again experience pleasure in serving the poor but
upon a real bond he built with the poor during his years of commitment to them. He serves them now because they are, in a real
sense, his family. He loves them not with the passion of first fervor but with the type of concern that one has for a family member. There is considerable emotional dryness in him, but, as time
passes, he has a growing sense of feeling at ease, comfortable, and
at home with the poor.

I do not know how his story will end. Perhaps he will serve
the poor in this way until he dies. If he does, he will die essentially
unselfish, living out in a good, though imperfect, fashion Christ's
preferential option for the poor. Perhaps, however, if he is given a
long life and much grace, he will, on the basis of the written word
of Scripture, at some point make a choice to serve the poor in a
way that goes beyond what practical wisdom and prudential
commitment demand. He will, then, like his counterparts in love
and prayer, enter the final stage of transformation to full maturity. The specific form that takes could vary. Perhaps he will go
off somewhere to work in the style of Mother Teresa; perhaps he
will live and work in a hospice center for cancer or AIDS victims;
or perhaps he will join L'Arche and spend the rest of his life living
with handicapped adults.

Whatever he does, that choice will initially bring him some
desolation and disorientation. Whatever moral securities he might
have built up during his previous years of service to the poor will
break down. He will spend some time, either long or short, unable
to reassure himself or give himself any practical hope. The only
reassurance and hope he will have will come to him through raw
faith in the word of God. He will be disconsolate, but he will not
turn back. Eventually a new day will dawn, and he will awake to
find that his passion has returned. He will be inflamed with a love

for the poor that dwarfs anything he felt all those years ago when he first converted. With that will come an overwhelming sense of the goodness and beauty not only of the poor but of all creation. He will live in a state of habitual joy and will, at moments, be unable to contain the sense of how good and beautiful it all is. He will have intermittent ecstasies, and they will be inflamed with a joy that no one will ever take away from him.

SOME CONCLUDING THOUGHTS

The French Renaissance philosopher Michel de Montaigne once wrote, "If you do not know how to die, never mind. Nature will tell you how to do it on the spot." For John of the Cross, that is also true in the way that nature, the natural unfolding of life, teaches us how to live. Whether the major focus of our lives is a certain relationship in love, a relationship to God in prayer, or a relationship to others through a generous giving of ourselves in service, if we remain faithful and endure its ups and downs, that relationship will transform us and bring us to maturity, meaning, and happiness. John was a faith-driven monk, so he traces this out through a movement of faith, but what he says is equally true for those who do not have an explicit faith but who give themselves over in altruism and fidelity to others through service in the world.

Again, consider the axiom in monasticism that says, "Stay in your cell and it will teach you all you need to know." The cell spoken of here is not a room in a monastery but the commitments we have made, the rooms in which we have chosen to put ourselves. We all have made vows: to one another, to God, and to ourselves. John of the Cross simply advises that we stay within those vows and accept the times of disillusionment—and then love, others, maturity, and God will find us.

ACKNOWLEDGMENTS

No book is the product of just one person. I need to express thanks to a lot of people for their help in bringing this book to birth.

Thanks to Image for shepherding this into publication and for their patience in waiting. A special thanks to Matthew Burdette, whose editorial mentoring made this a clearer text.

Thanks to JoAnne Chrones, my executive assistant, who for more than twenty-five years has kept me afloat and who today keeps me from drowning in the sea of social media and overextension.

A special thanks to Doug Mitchell, who, when he isn't composing folk songs or on tour, generously takes time to lay a hawk's eye to my writings and teach me the grammar I should have learned in high school.

Thanks to my four families: First, the community at Oblate School of Theology in San Antonio, Texas, supports me always and is my Eucharist community and my intellectual stimulus. Next, the religious community of which I am a member, the Missionary Oblates of Mary Immaculate, has for more than fifty years fed me, housed me, given me exceptional educational opportunities, and entrusted me with ministry. Then, not least, a large, amorphous tribe of biological family scattered throughout Canada gives me roots, gave me faith, taught me banter, and keeps teaching me about life. Finally, there are those who give me friendship, another amorphous tribe that keeps me sane and aware of what's important in life.

As well, I want to thank you, the reader, for picking up this book, a note in a milk bottle sent floating out into the open sea. A thousand thanks to all of you.

NOTES

||||||||||||||||||||||||||||||||

PREFACE

xiii **When Rachel Naomi Remen was fourteen years old.** Rachel Naomi Remen, *Kitchen Table Wisdom: Stories That Heal* (Riverhead, 1996), 23–25.

xvi **"Blessed are the pure in heart."** Matthew 5:8.

PART ONE

1 **"That is why I have decided."** Pablo d'Ors, *Biography of Silence: An Essay on Meditation,* trans. David Shook (Parallax, 2012), 103–4.

CHAPTER ONE

3 **"For everything there is a season."** Ecclesiastes 3:1.

4 **John of the Cross, using medieval and mystical terminology.** I recommend this edition: John of the Cross, *The Collected Works of St. John of the Cross,* 3rd ed., trans. Kieran Kavanaugh, OCD, and Otilio Rodriguez, OCD (ICS, 1991). Unfortunately there is no easy entry into understanding John of the Cross. He wrote five hundred years ago and is a very complex thinker who integrates personal experi-

ence, Scripture, mystical imagery, medieval piety, medieval vocabulary, aesthetic genius, church teaching, and personal holiness with Aristotle. It does not make for an easy read. I suggest entering his writings with the help of a trusted guide. I recommend Peter Tyler's *St John of the Cross* and Iain Matthew's *The Impact of God: Soundings from St John of the Cross.*

11   **It can be helpful to draw some perspectives.** A very helpful book on this is Germaine Greer, *The Change: Women, Ageing and the Menopause* (Alfred Knopf, 1991). Greer brilliantly traces the transition that nature intends here, a transition that takes in considerably more than the mere biological.

11   **They ask us to move from being.** To tease out what is contained in these rich concepts, I recommend the writings of James Hillman, Robert L. Moore, and Michael Meade.

12   **These struggles, John of the Cross says.** This is a theme in all of John of the Cross's works but can be seen more specifically in *The Dark Night,* book 2, chapters 1–3, in *Collected Works.*

12   **In one of his last books.** Henri J. M. Nouwen, *Our Greatest Gift: A Meditation on Dying and Caring* (HarperOne, 1994), xvi.

13   **Conversely, if we die at peace.** These insights are highlighted and fleshed out by Robert Ellsberg, *A Living Gospel: Reading God's Story in Holy Lives* (Orbis, 2019), 76–90.

13   **T. S. Eliot once said.** T. S. Eliot, "Little Gidding," in *Four Quartets* (Harcourt, 1943), 58.

CHAPTER TWO

14   **"The afternoon knows."** Swedish proverb.

14   **"Don't accept the modern myths of aging."** Lao Tzu, "We Are a River."

15   **James Hillman, in a brilliant book.** James Hillman, *The Force of Character: And the Lasting Life* (Ballantine, 1999).

15   "We can then imagine aging." Hillman, *The Force of Character,* xv.

15   "Earlier years must focus on." Hillman, *The Force of Character,* 56.

16   "Productivity is too narrow a measure." Hillman, *The Force of Character,* 16.

17   "'Old' is present in degrees." Hillman, *The Force of Character,* xxvi.

17   It sees *four* stages to our lives. For a quick but accurate synopsis of how Hinduism understands the stages of life, see Huston Smith, *The World's Religions* (HarperOne, 1991), 50–55.

17   In its view, these are the four essential stages. A number of institutes of spirituality and renewal centers are developing programs in Forest Dwelling—namely, programs aimed precisely at helping people ready their souls and form a vision for what they discern God is calling them to in their retirement years.

20   Among her many books. Germaine Greer, *The Change: Women, Ageing and the Menopause* (Alfred Knopf, 1991).

23   It is inviting her into. Greer purposefully dusts off an older term, *crone,* to refer to this stage in life, rather than a term like *Sophia,* fully aware the word "crone" is used pejoratively by most people. Her intent is to cleanse the word of that false pejorative connotation and restore it to its real meaning.

24   For Rohr, even though we may all reach. This is everywhere present, implicitly and explicitly, in Richard Rohr's writings and popular lectures. On this point, I recommend his work *Falling Upward: A Spirituality for the Two Halves of Life* (Jossey-Bass, 2011).

26   "Naked I came." Job 1:21.

27   A generation ago, Polish Swiss psychologist. Alice Miller, *The Drama of the Gifted Child: The Search for the True Self,* trans. Ruth Ward (Basic, 1997).

28 **In his book *The Second Mountain*.** David Brooks, *The Second Mountain: The Quest for a Moral Life* (Random House, 2019).

29 **Carl Jung once defined a vocation.** Brooks, *The Second Mountain*, 90.

29 **Frederick Buechner, the famed preacher, submits.** Brooks, *The Second Mountain*, 122.

30 **"My heart was full."** William Wordsworth, as quoted in Brooks, *The Second Mountain*, 92.

31 **As we age and move.** Brooks, *The Second Mountain*, 38.

31 **And all this, he says.** Brooks, *The Second Mountain*, 68.

31 **She was known and deeply respected.** Kathleen Dowling Singh, *The Grace in Living: Recognize It, Trust It, Abide in It* (Wisdom, 2016); Kathleen Dowling Singh, *The Grace in Aging: Awaken as You Grow Older* (Wisdom, 2014); Kathleen Dowling Singh, *The Grace in Dying: A Message of Hope, Comfort, and Spiritual Transformation* (HarperSanFrancisco, 1998).

CHAPTER THREE

34 **"The ultimate question that any of us."** Makoto Fujimura, *Silence and Beauty: Hidden Faith Born of Suffering* (InterVarsity, 2016), 208.

34 **The human aging process is designed.** James Hillman, *The Force of Character: And the Lasting Life* (Ballantine, 1999), xiii–xxi.

35 **When he was in his eighties.** Morris West, *A View from the Ridge: The Testimony of a Twentieth-Century Christian* (HarperOne, 1996).

36 **In 2007, William Young wrote a novel.** Wm. Paul Young, *The Shack: Where Tragedy Confronts Eternity* (Windblown Media, 2007).

37 **After teaching us the Lord's Prayer.** Matthew 6:12.

37 **He warns us that if we do not forgive.** Matthew 6:15.

38 **He summarizes it all in a short series of phrases.** Ira Byock,

The Four Things That Matter Most: A Book About Living (Atria, 2004), 3.

38 **Moreover, that rhythm is also.** For an explication of this, see Wayne Muller's fine work *Sabbath: Finding Rest, Renewal, and Delight in Our Busy Lives* (Bantam, 1999).

40 **Mystics call this breakdown.** The canonical voice on "dark nights of the soul" is the medieval mystic John of the Cross (1542–1591). All his works teach this. See John of the Cross, *The Collected Works of St. John of the Cross,* 3rd ed., trans. Kieran Kavanaugh, OCD, and Otilio Rodriguez, OCD (ICS, 1991). Also, it is for this reason that a failure of the imagination should not be confused with a loss of faith. Thus, for example, Charles Taylor, in his monumental work on secularity, suggests that today's radical drop in religious practice and the growing number of "nones" (people who claim to have no faith) is more a crisis of imagination than a crisis of faith. See Charles Taylor, *A Secular Age* (Belknap Press of Harvard University Press, 2007).

42 **As Saint Paul says.** 1 Corinthians 15:14.

42 **In the famous words of the mystic Julian of Norwich.** Julian of Norwich, *Revelations of Divine Love,* trans. Clifton Wolters (Penguin, 1966), 103. There is a quip attributed to Oscar Wilde that adds a clause to Julian's affirmation that in the end all will be well. Wilde is said to have added, "And if it isn't well, then it still is not the end!"

43 **I work as a chaplain.** Pierre Olivier Tremblay, in an oral presentation given at the Oblate School of Theology in 2010.

43 **As psychologist James Hollis points out.** James Hollis, *Living Between Worlds: Finding Personal Resilience in Changing Times* (Sounds True, 2020), 110, 119.

44 **Central to the message of Jesus.** Matthew 18:3.

47 **"No one takes [my life] from me."** John 10:18.

47 **"Father, into your hands."** Luke 23:46.

49   **Jesus's parable of the talents.** Matthew 25:14–30.

49   **Jesus teaches this explicitly.** John 14–17.

50   **In the Gospel of Mark.** Mark 1:15; cf. Matthew 4:17.

51   **Henri Nouwen captures this idea.** Henri J. M. Nouwen, *With Open Hands* (Ave Maria, 1972).

PART TWO

53   **"When the signs of age begin."** Pierre Teilhard de Chardin, *Le Milieu Divin: An Essay on the Interior Life* (William Collins Sons and Co., 1960), 69–70.

CHAPTER FOUR

55   **What unique perspectives?** An apologia is in order here. This chapter is partly a repetition of chapter 9 in my previous book *Sacred Fire.* When I wrote *Sacred Fire,* I was trying to outline a spirituality of how to give one's life away; I ended it with what I then called an Anticipatory Incompletion—namely, a closing chapter highlighting the essence of what appears in this book. This chapter is largely a repetition of that chapter. As well, much of the material in this chapter was also published in Ronald Rolheiser, OMI, "Insane for the Light: The Final Stage of Human Maturity and Christian Discipleship," *Chicago Studies* 52, no. 2 (2013).

56   **Indeed, in three of the Gospels.** This is true for the Synoptic Gospels: Matthew, Mark, and Luke. Things are very different in John's Gospel. Throughout his entire Gospel, John emphasizes the divinity of Jesus, to the point of leaving almost no humanity in him. This carries through to John's narrative of the Passion, where he has Jesus in full control, showing no human weakness whatsoever. John's passion narrative puts emphasis on the trial of Jesus, and John writes it in such a way that everyone *except* Jesus is on trial, including us, the readers.

57 **He is passive, a patient.** For an excellent, detailed, and scholarly analysis of this see W. H. Vanstone, *The Stature of Waiting* (Morehouse, 1982).

57 **As Nouwen approached the bed.** Henri Nouwen, *Spirituality of Waiting: Being Alert to God's Presence in our Lives*, *Audio Cassette* (Ave Maria, 2006). The dialogue here is a not an exact verbatim but a "rendering" of the substance of the conversation.

58 **Among other things, Nouwen read the passion narratives.** Nouwen also read aloud to him W. H. Vanstone's book *The Stature of Waiting*.

62 **The Gospel of John tells us.** John 19:34.

63 **"I'm a stone's throw away from everyone."** Luke 22:41–45.

64 **When Jesus is saying farewell to his disciples.** John 14–17. In each of the other three Gospels, the Last Supper is recorded very briefly, in a paragraph or two. In John's Gospel, Jesus's farewell discourse at the Last Supper constitutes about half of his entire Gospel. And in that farewell speech, Jesus says again and again that it is better for his disciples that he goes away; otherwise, they will not be able to receive the gift of his spirit.

CHAPTER FIVE

69 **The renowned spiritual writer Henri Nouwen.** Henri J. M. Nouwen, *In Memoriam* (Ave Maria, 1980).

71 **"I once thought that the difference."** Michael J. Buckley, *What Do You Seek? The Questions of Jesus as Challenge and Promise* (Eerdmans, 2016), 85.

71 **In the view of Kathleen Dowling Singh.** Singh offers an observation, based on being present when dozens of people have died. She submits that if you watch very closely as someone is dying, you will observe that often, perhaps most times, the person goes into ecstasy in the last seconds of his

life. Singh suggests that this is because he is breaking into
the reality of spirit.

71   **Shortly before he dies on the cross.** Matthew 27:46; Mark
15:34.

73   **Thomas Keating, the renowned spiritual writer.** Thomas
Keating, private conversation with author.

73   *Unanimity minus one.* Mark 14:32–37; Luke 22:39–46.

75   **In God, "we live and move and have our being."** Acts 17:28.

79   **Jesus cries out.** Matthew 27:46; Mark 15:34.

80   **Paul's desolation in 2 Corinthians.** 2 Corinthians 4.

80   **He tells his religious superior.** Ursula King, *Spirit of Fire:
The Life and Vision of Teilhard de Chardin* (Orbis, 1996), 210.

81   **Recognize the wisdom given.** Lamentations 3:29.

81   *Accept the unknowing.* John of the Cross, *The Collected
Works of St. John of the Cross,* 3rd ed., trans. Kieran Kavanaugh, OCD, and Otilio Rodriguez, OCD (ICS, 1991). This
concept is central in book 2 of *The Dark Night.*

85   **Thérèse of Lisieux once said.** Thérèse of Lisieux, *Story of a
Soul: The Autobiography of Saint Thérèse of Lisieux,* 3rd ed.,
trans. John Clarke, OCD (ICS, 1975).

85   **The great Spanish doctor.** John of the Cross, "The Dark
Night," book 2, chapters 1–4.

87   **Renowned spiritual author Michael J. Buckley.** For a
shorter, succinct thesis on this, see Michael J. Buckley,
"Atheism and Contemplation," *Theological Studies* 40, no.
4 (December 1, 1979), 680–99, https://theologicalstudies.net
/wp-content/uploads/2022/08/40.4.2.pdf. For a major scholarly analysis, see Michael J. Buckley, *At the Origins of Modern
Atheism* (Yale University Press, 1987).

PART THREE

89   **"The developmental tasks of late life."** Connie Zweig, *The
Inner Work of Age: Shifting from Role to Soul* (Park Street,
2021), 109.

CHAPTER SIX

91   **"God is being built."** Nikos Kazantzakis, *Report to Greco,* trans. P. A. Bien (Simon and Schuster, 1965), 18.

98   **We are to name.** Luke 4:18.

99   **It invites us, like Jesus.** Luke 19:41–42.

99   **Be compassionate in the same manner.** Luke 6:36. It is interesting to note that in Matthew's Gospel, Jesus says not "be compassionate" but "be perfect . . . as your heavenly Father is perfect" (5:48). That is easily misunderstood from our mindset, where perfect means having no flaws. That, of course, is an impossible ideal for us humans. But for Jesus, a first-century Hebrew, the word "perfect" meant "compassion."

100 **He loves them even in their distance from him.** Luke 15. This is the parable of the prodigal son and the older brother.

103 **Christianity, as Marilynne Robinson says.** Marilynne Robinson, *When I Was a Child I Read Books* (Farrar, Straus and Giroux, 2012), 141.

104 **What is a blessing?** In a previous book, I offer an extensive development on the notion of blessing. See Ronald Rolheiser, *Sacred Fire: A Vision for a Deeper Human and Christian Maturity* (Image, 2014).

109 **G. K. Chesterton once quipped.** G. K. Chesterton, *The Everlasting Man* (Dodd, Mead, 1925), 182.

109 **The philosopher Eric Mascall.** Mascall's verbatim comment: "We shall never become theists if we take the world for granted; but so long as we do *not* take it for granted we are within measurable distance of taking it as granted to us by God." E. L. Mascall, *Existence and Analogy* (Longmans, Green, 1949), 85.

110 **What is the endgame of moving.** Connie Zweig, *The Inner Work of Age: Shifting from Role to Soul* (Park Street, 2021).

CHAPTER SEVEN

111   **"A whole lifetime is needed."** Seneca, *How to Die: An Ancient Guide to the End of Life,* ed. and trans. James S. Romm (Princeton University Press, 2018), xx.

111   **I single out for special mention the memoirs.** See the bibliography for their books.

112   **And from a purely secular perspective.** For insight into how a number of famous persons, including Susan Sontag, Sigmund Freud, John Updike, and Dylan Thomas, faced their deaths, see Katie Roiphe, *The Violet Hour: Great Writers at the End* (Dial, 2016). See also Erica Jong, *Fear of Dying* (St. Martin's, 2015).

117   **He was born in Spain in 1542.** A brief biography of John is given in chapter 9. His complete works can be found in one volume: John of the Cross, *The Collected Works of St. John of the Cross,* 3rd ed., trans. Kieran Kavanaugh, OCD, and Otilio Rodriguez, OCD (ICS, 1991).

117   **John believed that we have three natural faculties.** In the terminology of his time, the word "memory" did not have the connotations it has today—that is, as a faculty that remembers. Rather, it referred to the deepest part of us, something beyond the conscious ego, something that today we might call the "gut" or the "person." For John and for medieval anthropology, the idea was that we think with our heads and we feel with our hearts, but who does the thinking and the feeling? It is the part of us that sits behind the head and the heart and does the remembering; hence, they called it the "memory."

121   **John, however, also offers us a proactive way.** John's prescriptions for this are given in *The Ascent of Mount Carmel,* book 2, chapters 5–6, in *Collected Works.*

121   **Jesus, as we know, promised.** Matthew 5:8.

122   **In that consummation.** See John of the Cross, *The Living Flame of Love,* in *Collected Works.*

122   **Nouwen was one of the first.** Henri J. M. Nouwen, *Our Greatest Gift: A Meditation on Dying and Caring* (HarperOne, 1994), xvi–xvii.

124   **His wound was essentially healed.** For example, see the book that is considered his masterpiece: Henri J. M. Nouwen, *The Return of the Prodigal Son: A Meditation on Fathers, Brothers, and Sons* (Doubleday, 1992).

125   **A brilliant exposé of this.** Frederick Buechner, *The Magnificent Defeat* (Seabury, 1966), 18.

125   **Jacob wrestling with a stranger.** Genesis 32:22–32.

125   **Buechner comments.** Buechner, *The Magnificent Defeat,* 18.

128   **When the prophet Elijah was dying.** 2 Kings 2:9.

129   **The first is the Greek writer Nikos Kazantzakis.** Nikos Kazantzakis, *Report to Greco,* trans. P. A. Bien (Simon and Schuster, 1965), 17.

129   **The second stoic I recommend is Nina Riggs.** Nina Riggs, *The Bright Hour: A Memoir of Living and Dying* (Simon and Schuster, 2017).

130   **The late Ivan Illich, the Austrian theologian.** This saying is attributed to Ivan Illich, though I have never been able to track down the specific reference.

CHAPTER EIGHT

132   **"What no eye has seen."** 1 Corinthians 2:9.

133   **Today there is an ever-expanding body of literature.** See, for example, Eben Alexander, *Proof of Heaven: A Neurosurgeon's Journey into the Afterlife* (Simon and Schuster, 2012); Raymond A. Moody, Jr., *Life After Life* (Bantam, 1975); and numerous others.

133   **Isaiah suggests that in heaven.** Isaiah 11:6–7; 25:6.

134   **Andrew Greeley once folded these images.** Andrew M. Greeley, *Life for a Wanderer* (Doubleday, 1969), 161–62.

134   **They believe that in the ecstasy of heaven.** It is on this point that Christians, Jews, and Muslims differ from many Hindus and Buddhists.

135   **The final triumph of God and of goodness.** Among others, the great patristic theologian Gregory of Nyssa (ca. 335—ca. 395) hints at this.

137   **The Gospels tell us there is a sin.** Matthew 12:31–32.

138   **Fruit of the Holy Spirit.** Galatians 5:22–23.

142   **"The tombs also were opened."** Matthew 27:50–52.

142   **"Why are you looking for a live person in a cemetery?"** Luke 24:5; Mark 16:6–7.

144   **When Karl Rahner says that for everyone.** Karl Rahner, *Servants of the Lord* (Herder and Herder, 1968), 152.

145   **G. K. Chesterton once said that Christianity.** G. K. Chesterton, *Orthodoxy* (Relevant, 2006), 84.

PART FOUR

151   **"To reach satisfaction in all."** Michel de Montaigne, quoted in Kieran Setiya, *Midlife: A Philosophical Guide* (Princeton University Press, 2017), 106.

CHAPTER NINE

153   **"First comes falling in love."** Michael Leach, quoted in Sister Wendy Beckett and Robert Ellsberg, *Dearest Sister Wendy: A Surprising Story of Faith and Friendship* (Orbis, 2022), 170.

155   **His commentaries on his poems.** John wrote four major books: *The Ascent of Mount Carmel, The Dark Night, The Spiritual Canticle,* and *The Living Flame of Love.* As well, he wrote poems, maxims, counsels, and letters. All these can found in John of the Cross, *The Collected Works of St. John*

of the Cross, 3rd ed., trans. Kieran Kavanaugh, OCD, and Otilio Rodriguez, OCD (ICS, 1991).

170 **As the author of Lamentations says.** Lamentations 3:29.

174 **The French Renaissance philosopher Michel de Montaigne.** Michel de Montaigne, quoted in Kieran Setiya, *Midlife: A Philosophical Guide* (Princeton University Press, 2017), 106.

SELECTED BIBLIOGRAPHY

Aronson, Louise. *Elderhood: Redefining Aging, Transforming Medicine, Reimagining Life*. Bloomsbury, 2019.

Atwood, Margaret. *Dearly: New Poems*. Ecco, 2020.

Au, Wilkie, and Noreen Cannon Au. *Aging with Wisdom and Grace*. Paulist, 2019.

Bernardin, Joseph Cardinal. *The Gift of Peace: Personal Reflections*. Loyola, 1997.

Bourgeault, Cynthia. *Love Is Stronger Than Death: The Mystical Union of Two Souls*. Monkfish, 1997.

Bowler, Kate. *Everything Happens for a Reason: And Other Lies I've Loved*. Random House, 2018.

Brooks, Arthur C. *From Strength to Strength: Finding Success, Happiness, and Deep Purpose in the Second Half of Life*. Portfolio/Penguin, 2022.

Brooks, David. *The Second Mountain: The Quest for a Moral Life*. Random House, 2019.

Byock, Ira. *Dying Well: Peace and Possibilities at the End of Life*. Riverhead, 1997.

Byock, Ira, *The Four Things That Matter Most: A Book About Living*. Atria, 2004.

Cain, Bill, *The Book of Cain: On Adding a New Book to the Family Bible*. Orbis, 2023.

Cicero, Marcus Tullius. *On Old Age*. Translation from the original Latin is available online at The Ethics of Suicide Digital Archive. May 15, 2015. https://ethicsofsuicide.lib.utah.edu/selections/cicero.

Cohen, Leonard. *You Want It Darker*. Produced by Adam Cohen and Patrick Leonard. Columbia Records. Released October 21, 2016.

Cunningham, Frank J. *Vesper Time: The Spiritual Practice of Growing Older*. Orbis, 2017.

Danticat, Edwidge. *The Art of Death: Writing the Final Story*. Graywolf, 2017.

D'Arcy, Paula, *Gift of the Red Bird: The Story of a Divine Encounter*. Crossroad, 1996.

Downey, Michael. *The Depth of God's Reach: A Spirituality of Christ's Descent*. Orbis, 2018.

Ephron, Nora. *I Remember Nothing: And Other Reflections*. Vintage, 2010.

Gallagher, Michael Paul. *Into Extra Time: Living Through the Final Stages of Cancer and Jottings Along the Way*. Darton, Longman & Todd, 2016.

Hillman, James. *The Force of Character: And the Lasting Life*. Ballantine, 1999.

Hollis, James. *Living Between Worlds: Finding Personal Resilience in Changing Times*. Sounds True, 2020.

Jong, Erica. *Fear of Dying*. St. Martin's, 2015.

Kalanithi, Paul. *When Breath Becomes Air*. Random House, 2016.

Kalina, Kathy. *Midwife for Souls: Spiritual Care for the Dying*. Pauline, 1993.

Kazantzakis, Nikos. *Report to Greco*. Translated by P. A. Bien. Simon and Schuster, 1965.

Lebreton, Christophe. *Born from the Gaze of God: The Tibhirine Journal of a Martyr Monk, 1993–1996*. Translated by Mette Louise Nygård and Edith Scholl. Liturgical, 2014.

Lewis, C. S. *The Great Divorce*. Fount, 1946. Today available from multiple publishers.

McEntyre, Marilyn Chandler. *A Faithful Farewell: Living Your Last Chapter with Love*. Eerdmans, 2015.

Miller, Alice. *The Drama of the Gifted Child: The Search for the True Self*. Translated by Ruth Ward. Basic, 1981.

Moore, Thomas. *Ageless Soul: The Lifelong Journey Toward Meaning and Joy*. St. Martin's, 2017.

Moriarty, John. *Serious Sounds*. Lilliput, 2007.

Nicholl, Donald. *The Testing of Hearts: A Pilgrim's Journey*. 2nd ed. Edited by Adrian Hastings. Darton, Longman & Todd, 1998.

Nouwen, Henri J. M., and Walter J. Gaffney. *Aging: The Fulfillment of Life*. Image, 1974.

Nouwen, Henri J. M. *Beyond the Mirror: Reflections on Death and Life*. Crossroad, 2001.

Nouwen, Henri J. M. *The Dance of Life: Weaving Sorrows and Blessings into One Joyful Step*. Edited by Michael Ford. Ave Maria, 2005.

Nouwen, Henri J. M. *In Memoriam*. Ave Maria, 1980.

Nouwen, Henri J. M. *Our Greatest Gift: A Meditation on Dying and Caring*. HarperOne, 1994.

Nouwen, Henri J. M. *The Return of the Prodigal Son: A Meditation on Fathers, Brothers, and Sons.* Doubleday, 1992.

O'Leary, Daniel. *Dancing to My Death: With the Love Called Cancer.* Columba, 2019.

Olivera, Bernardo. *How Far to Follow? The Martyrs of Atlas.* Saint Bede's, 1997.

O'Rourke, Michelle. *Befriending Death: Henri Nouwen and a Spirituality of Dying.* Orbis, 2009.

Palmer, Parker J. *On the Brink of Everything: Grace, Gravity, and Getting Old.* Berrett-Koehler, 2018.

Rappaport, Nancy. *In Her Wake: A Child Psychiatrist Explores the Mystery of Her Mother's Suicide.* Basic, 2009.

Remen, Rachel Naomi. *Kitchen Table Wisdom: Stories That Heal.* Riverhead, 1996.

Renkl, Margaret. *Late Migrations: A Natural History of Love and Loss.* Milkweed Editions, 2019.

Riggs, Nina. *The Bright Hour: A Memoir of Living and Dying.* Simon and Schuster, 2017.

Robinson, Marilynne. *When I Was a Child I Read Books.* Farrar, Straus and Giroux, 2012.

Rohr, Richard. *Falling Upward: A Spirituality for the Two Halves of Life.* Jossey-Bass, 2011.

Roiphe, Katie. *The Violet Hour: Great Writers at the End.* Dial, 2016.

Seneca, *How to Die: An Ancient Guide to the End of Life.* Edited and translated by James S. Romm. Princeton University Press, 2018.

Setiya, Kieran. *Midlife: A Philosophical Guide.* Princeton University Press, 2017.

Sheehan, Martina Lehane. *Waiting in Mindful Hope.* Veritas, 2017.

Singh, Kathleen Dowling. *The Grace in Aging: Awaken as You Grow Older*. Wisdom, 2014.

Singh, Kathleen Dowling. *The Grace in Dying: A Message of Hope, Comfort, and Spiritual Transformation*. HarperSanFrancisco, 1998.

Singh, Kathleen Dowling. *The Grace in Living: Recognize It, Trust It, Abide in It*. Wisdom, 2016.

Smith, Carol Ann, and Eugene F. Merz. *Moments to Remember: Ignatian Wisdom for Aging*. New City Press, 2015.

Vandekerckhove, Bieke. *The Taste of Silence: How I Came to Be at Home with Myself*. Translated by Rudolf V. Van Puymbroeck. Liturgical, 2015.

Vanstone, W. H. *The Stature of Waiting*. Morehouse, 1982.

Viorst, Judith. *Suddenly Sixty: And Other Shocks of Later Life*. Simon and Schuster, 2000.

West, Morris. *A View from the Ridge: The Testimony of a Twentieth-Century Christian*. HarperOne, 1996.

Witherup, Ronald D. *What Does the Bible Say About Old Age?* New City Press, 2019.

Yungblut, John. *On Hallowing One's Dimishments*. Pendle Hill, 1990.

Zweig, Connie. *The Inner Work of Age: Shifting from Role to Soul*. Park Street, 2021.

ABOUT THE AUTHOR

RONALD ROLHEISER is a specialist in the fields of spirituality and systematic theology. He is president emeritus of the Oblate School of Theology in San Antonio, Texas, and a professor of spirituality there. His books, notably *The Restless Heart, The Holy Longing,* and *Sacred Fire,* are popular throughout the English-speaking world and have now been translated into many languages. His weekly column is carried by more than eighty newspapers worldwide.

ABOUT THE TYPE

This book was set in Granjon, a modern recutting of a typeface produced under the direction of George W. Jones (1860–1942), who based Granjon's design upon the letterforms of Claude Garamond (1480–1561). The name was given to the typeface as a tribute to the typographic designer Robert Granjon (1513–89).

Also from bestselling author Ronald Rolheiser

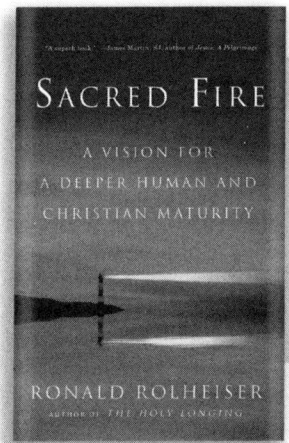

With his trademark acuity, wit, and thoughtfulness, Rolheiser shows how identifying and embracing discipleship will lead to new heights of spiritual awareness and maturity.

Channeling the deep, mysterious desires of our hearts, Ronald Rolheiser leads readers from restlessness to peace, showing a contemporary path to an authentic and healthy spiritual life.

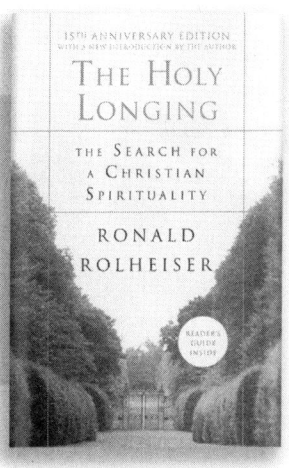

Learn more about Ronald Rolheiser's books at
penguinrandomhouse.com.

IMAGE